KEEPING SAFE AND WORKING EFFECTIVELY

FOR SOCIAL WORKERS AND HEALTH PROFESSIONALS

KEEPING SAFE AND WORKING EFFECTIVELY

FOR SOCIAL WORKERS AND HEALTH PROFESSIONALS

Brian Atkins

Second Edition

Routledge
Taylor & Francis Group

LONDON AND NEW YORK

CRITICAL
SKILLS FOR
SOCIAL WORK

First edition published in 2013 by Critical Publishing Ltd.

Second edition published 2023

Published 2025 by Routledge
4 Park Square, Milton Park, Abingdon, Oxon OX14 4RN
605 Third Avenue, New York, NY 10017

Routledge is an imprint of the Taylor & Francis Group, an informa business

British Library Cataloguing in Publication Data
A CIP record for this book is available from the British Library

ISBN: 9781915713339 (pbk)
ISBN: 9781041055907 (ebk)

Cover design by Greensplash Limited

DOI: 10.4324/9781041055907

Contents

About the author   viii

Introduction to the Second Edition   1

1. The extent of violence against social care workers and health professionals   3

Introduction   3
Current examples of work-related intimidation, threat and violence   3
Violence against health professionals   6
Impact on practice   7
Impact on the performance of social care organisations   8
What has been done to address this issue?   9
Is the situation getting better?   9

2. The physiological and psychological impact of violence and intimidation on professional decision-making   16

Introduction   16
Immediate, unexpected threats or aggression   16
Violence and aggression in response to triggers   17
Long-term intimidation and realistic threats of violence
    within the professional/client relationship   17
Physiological responses to threats and violence   17
Working with violent and aggressive families   19
Job context   20
The importance of the professional relationship   22
The question of power   23
Hostage theory   24
Stockholm syndrome   25
Impact on protective workers   26
Coping strategies   26
Differences between terrorist hostage and child protection situations   27
The broader impact of hostage relationships on work effectiveness   27
Research findings   28
What are the implications for practice and for employers?   28

3. What practitioners can do to keep themselves safe   31

    Introduction   31
    Safety awareness   31
    Risk assessments   35
    Teamwork   38
    Building on training   39
    Responsibilities of staff   40

4. What organisations can do to keep staff safe   42

    Why social care and health organisations should keep their staff safe   42
    Key questions for employers   42
    Job design   43
    The duty of care for employers   43
    Key responsibilities of employers   44
    Supervision   45
    Planning interventions   46
    Team working   47
    Lone working and staff safety policies   48
    Employer's self-audit   48
    Single- and multi-agency working practices   52
    Training in working safely   52

5. Keeping safe in an incident   55

    Introduction   55
    The causes of violent and aggressive behaviour   55
    What the behaviour is trying to achieve   57
    Functional Behavioural Analysis   57
    Expressions of violence and aggression   58
    Trauma-informed practice and strengths-based approaches   58
    The cycle of emotional arousal   59
    The physiology of stress: what is actually happening to the body when
        it is under stress?   62
    Body language and non-verbal communication   63
    How our own behaviour can affect outcomes   64
    Batari's box   64
    Recognising and using body language for personal safety: distinguishing
        between warning and danger signs   65
    What can you do to protect yourself and manage situations of aggression
        and violence?   67
    Responding to aggressive and violent behaviour assertively   70
    Effective resolution versus winning   71
    Note   75

6.	**Post-incident responses**	**76**
	Introduction	76
	Duty of care to staff	79
7.	**Working with highly resistant families**	**83**
	Introduction	83
	Types of resistance	83
	Working with resistant families	84
	Strengths-based approaches	87
8.	**Working in non-responsive institutions**	**90**
	Introduction	90
	Workplace culture	90
	UNISON	91
	Government documents and codes of practice	92
	What you can do as a practitioner in health or social care	92
9.	**Performance management in social care**	**95**
	Introduction	95
	Performance management in relation to staff safety	96
	Organisational performance	97
	Core groups	99
	Courts and care proceedings	100
10.	**Working effectively in stressful situations: putting it all together**	**101**
	A framework for safe and effective working	101
11.	**Summary of issues**	**106**
	Final thoughts	106
	Summary of chapters	106
	Bibliography	110
	Index	114

About the author

 **Brian Atkins** BSc, CQSW, MBA is an experienced social work practitioner and manager and has worked in a range of social care services including children's services fieldwork, child protection, residential care, leaving care services, family placement and youth offending. He has also worked as a policy and planning manager with an English local authority.

In his later career, Brian worked as an independent consultant with public, voluntary and independent sector social care organisations across England and Wales. His consultancy experience included service review in a range of settings, including child protection, children in care, criminal justice partnerships, youth offending and disability, including learning difficulties. He has also led in the development of service user empowerment programmes, on systems review projects in social care and health organisations and in the construction of statutory plans.

Brian has had a long term interest in improving the safety of professionals doing their job in challenging situations, deriving from personal experience and observing the impact on colleagues. He has worked as a trainer and consultant in personal safety for professionals, and worked with institutions to reduce the need for physical interventions in residential and day care environments.

Introduction to the Second Edition

This book is a development of my original book *Personal Safety for Social Workers and Health Professionals* published in 2013. Although this second edition contains much of the original material it has been updated to take into account new developments, in particular the impact of working online, using social media and working with vulnerable adolescents subject to exploitation.

The original book focused on helping professionals keep safe in stressful situations involving intimidation and threats from the people and families they work with.

The new book takes this aim a stage further. The focus of this edition is not just helping social work professionals to stay safe, but also to help them and their teams work effectively in protecting children and vulnerable adults in these challenging situations. This, after all, is why social workers are in these situations in the first place.

In preparation for this edition, I have held meetings with social workers and their managers across a range of children's services, in particular those dealing with child protection and working with adolescents at risk of exploitation. I've talked to managers from a range of different local authorities, to workers and managers from adult social care, and with health professionals dealing with mental health issues – all workplaces which have been associated with particularly challenging issues.

What is clear from these consultations is that threats and intimidation to social workers and associated health professionals remain a very real issue, and one which affects both assessment and decision-making, and also the employing organisation's ability to recruit and retain workers.

It is also evident that there are wide differences in the way organisations respond to this issue. In a minority of organisations, professionals can be left to deal with the issues as best they can, through their own devices, although receiving emotional support from their supervisors.

In other organisations, a well-worked-out strategy is in place, proactively identifying risks in specific situations and planning with staff to respond to them and to implement specific strategies to keep both their staff and clients safe.

This proactive response is a key theme of this edition, which can both help to protect staff and enable them to work effectively in the protection of the children and vulnerable adults with whom they work.

The timing of the publication of this edition is fortunate in that it can be used to influence and support the training programmes currently being promised by the government to support social workers in their challenging task. It could also help to improve the outcomes for the children and others at risk from challenging living situations.

It is my hope that this book will help individual professionals both to keep safe and to be able to work effectively in threatening and challenging situations. It could also help employing organisations to be more aware of these issues and support them to develop strategies to improve the well-being of staff and improve outcomes for those being protected by their services.

Brian Atkins, 2023

DEDICATION

To Ann White, Dino Armagan and Maggie Beer for their work in developing much of the practical material in this book.

The extent of violence against social care workers and health professionals

INTRODUCTION

In the first edition of this book, I highlighted examples of violence and intimidating behaviour against social care professionals using examples from 1997 to 2012. In this current edition, I provide worrying evidence that this has continued, and indeed increased in prevalence. In widening the context of the work, in particular work with vulnerable adolescents, and in the technology used, including social media and online working, the impact on the mental health, living arrangements and professional competence of professionals continues to be significant.

CURRENT EXAMPLES OF WORK-RELATED INTIMIDATION, THREAT AND VIOLENCE

Graphic examples of this are provided in the excellent report from BASW Northern Ireland (2018). This report was based on a survey of all registered social workers in Northern Ireland and received over 220 responses; 51 per cent were from children and family services, 14 per cent from mental health services, 10 per cent from criminal justice, 12 per cent from disability and 7 per cent from older people services.

Intimidating behaviour

Of the respondents to the BASW Northern Ireland survey, 86 per cent had experienced intimidating behaviour, including, more recently, through social media. Examples of this include the following.

- Respondents recounted a growth in abuse via social media, with examples given of service users or their family members spreading false and malicious information about social workers via Facebook pages and YouTube.

- Associated with but not limited to this activity were accounts of social workers having home visits video-recorded and photographs taken of them or their vehicles, which was noted to cause significant stress and anxiety.

- Implied threats included service users referring to personal information about social workers, for example detailing knowledge of their home address, car registration or information about their children's schools. Examples were also provided of service users loitering outside social work offices, as were cases of service users following social workers or their family members in their cars.

The client told me he had walked every street in my development until he found my car outside my house. He was being challenged about his increased risk towards others and took the opportunity to tell me that he had my details. While he was not explicit in his threats, the language used and what was said left me believing that this man could hurt me and he had a history of intimidation and harm to those he perceived had wronged him.

(Criminal Justice Social Worker, BASW Northern Ireland, 2018, p 8)

In my role as an Approved Social Worker, when assessing a patient, other family members were present and appeared to intimate a threat of physical violence by walking past me with a baseball bat which they were hitting against their hands.

(Older People's Social Worker, BASW Northern Ireland, 2018, p 8)

An issue frequently cited as intimidating by respondents was the misuse of complaints processes. This was highlighted as a key factor in undermining social workers' confidence in performing their duties. Information was also provided concerning service users using information regarding social workers' personal circumstances or phobias in attempt to discredit and undermine them.

Threats

Three-quarters (75 per cent) of respondents stated that in their role as a social worker they had experienced a threat of violence made against them, or a family member, in person or by telephone. The nature of many of the threats received are deeply shocking. Respondents noted receiving death threats, threats to torture and threats to rape. While most frequently directed at social workers, threats of these type were also intended for the partners and children of social workers. Social workers recounted incidents of being constantly harassed or stalked, and threats of damage to their cars or property. Examples were also given of social workers being threatened with sexual violence, both in person and via text message.

Social media was highlighted as playing a role in enabling threats against social workers.

In Northern Ireland there was also the context of threats associated with paramilitary organisations.

Violence

Exactly half (50 per cent) of all social workers who participated in the survey explained they had been subjected to physical violence. Physical assault is the form of violence respondents were most likely to have experienced; 42 per cent of respondents reported being physically assaulted at least once.

Social workers recounted multiple incidents of being subjected to physical assault. Examples of the violence experienced include: being pulled to the floor and kicked in the head, being punched in the face, being grabbed by the throat and choked, being bitten, having bones broken, and being pushed around and manhandled. Respondents also recounted experiences of being attacked with knives or improvised weapons, for example, chairs, fire extinguishers, and hot liquids. Numerous incidents of being spat upon were cited in social workers' responses.

Impact

The most prevalent consequence of intimidation, threats and violence is a detrimental impact on social workers' emotional well-being; 93 per cent of those who had experienced intimidation, 86 per cent of those who were subjected to threats, and 94 per cent who experienced violence reported a detrimental impact in this area.

Finally, a detrimental impact to family life and relationships is most frequently experienced by social workers who have been subjected to physical violence. Three-quarters (75 per cent) of social workers who experienced violence reported a detrimental impact.

Examples were given of social workers being frightened to come to work, feeling a sense of dread, and being unable to socialise in the locality they worked in. Cases were also cited of social workers fearing they and their families would be physically attacked.

> *At times it has felt as if the Trust's view of assaults on residential social workers is that this is part and parcel of the job… At times I have dreaded coming into work for more of the same. It can create apathy and a sense of helplessness in the team. I feel this has significantly impacted upon my well-being through long periods of managing inappropriate levels of stress.*
>
> (Residential Children's Service Social Worker,
> BASW Northern Ireland, 2018, p 14)

> *I think there is an unacceptable 'acceptance' that violence and aggression is all par for the course for social workers working in the area of child protection.*
>
> (Children and Families Social Worker,
> BASW Northern Ireland, 2018, p 16)

Examples from England and Wales

In England and Wales, the UK Health and Safety Executive's (2022) Violence at Work statistics show that health and social care specialists are at much higher risk of assaults and threats at work than the general population, second only to 'protective service workers' such as police and firefighters. Its data is based on the national crime survey and showed 5.1 per cent of health and social care workers suffered an incident of violence at work, compared to 1.4 per cent average across all sectors of the working population.

The impact of threats and potential violence on professionals has been highlighted in the recent high profile cases of Arthur Labinjo-Hughes and Star Hobson which led to a major review of children's social work practice.

The headline of a report in Social Work News stated that *'Social workers have had to leave their homes because of abuse and threats following the trial of Arthur Labinjo-Hughes's killers, a council boss has said'* (Social Work News, 2022). Nick Page, chief executive of Solihull Council, said the murder of the six-year-old in June 2020 had *'devastated'* the community, but went on to add he was concerned by the level of abuse and threats towards social workers in the aftermath, which saw some having to leave their own homes. In a video statement responding to the review, Mr Page said: *'What I'm clear about is that social work, being a social worker, is one of the most caring, yet hardest vocations to do'* (Social Work News, 2022).

Outside the UK

The situation is not unique to the UK. For example, in 2018 in the United States the Bureau of Labor Statistics (2020) found that health and social service workers were nearly five times as likely to suffer a serious workplace violence injury than workers in other sectors. Social workers and healthcare professionals provide essential mental health and health services to individuals and groups in a wide variety of settings such as hospitals, home care agencies, child welfare departments, community-based clinics, and schools. Social workers face unique vulnerabilities at work, as they typically provide services outside the four walls of an office, such as in client homes and community-based settings.

Far too many social workers and health professionals have lost their lives to workplace violence. The alarming statistics do not capture the substantial number of unreported assaults, which, according to one survey, are as high as 85 per cent of all assaults (AFGE, 2016).

VIOLENCE AGAINST HEALTH PROFESSIONALS

The NHS (2021) Staff Survey, of which there were nearly 600,000 responses from 220 NHS trusts, found that:

- 14.3 per cent of NHS staff have experienced at least one incident of physical violence from patients, service users, relatives or other members of the public in the last 12 months. In the ambulance sector, our paramedics have experienced a much higher volume of abuse (31.4 per cent);

- the impact on staff is significant, with violent attacks contributing to 46.8 per cent of staff feeling unwell as a result of work-related stress in the last 12 months, and with 31.1 per cent thinking about leaving the organisation.

The NHS has had a zero tolerance policy towards violence to staff since 1999, and there has been a significant increase in the number of offenders being prosecuted since 2003, when the Counter Fraud and Security Management Service (CFSMS) was set up.

In 2021 a survey carried out for the Healthcare Commission showed that 14.3 per cent of staff across all trusts reported having been physically assaulted by patients in the previous 12 months (NHS, 2021).

Twenty-eight per cent of frontline staff had experienced this abuse from patients or patients' relatives. The survey showed an overall 5 per cent increase in the reporting of violence and abuse, and a 3 per cent increase in staff who feel that their Trust would take effective action if staff were physically attacked by patients, relatives or other members of the public.

Health professionals, including health visitors, midwives, mental health nurses, GPs and consultants, experience many of the same threats as social workers, particularly when working in the field of child protection, and in contexts where they visit service users in their own homes.

Up to 100,000 healthcare professionals are working on their own in the NHS every day.

IMPACT ON PRACTICE

Violence and aggression from service users can affect protective workers' judgement and ability to work with confidence in family situations. This has been highlighted by many child death enquiry reports going back to Victoria Climbié and earlier. Lord Laming, in his report on the death of Victoria Climbié, said:

I recognise that those who take on the work of protecting children at risk of deliberate harm face a tough and challenging task. Staff doing this work need a combination of professional skills and personal qualities, not least of which are persistence and courage. Adults who deliberately exploit the vulnerability of children can behave in devious and menacing ways.

(Lord Laming 2003, p 3)

The parents of Ainlee Walker were sentenced to long terms of imprisonment for the manslaughter of their daughter. They were aggressive and violent towards child protection staff, and the social workers and health visitors involved became '*paralysed by fear*' (*Guardian*, 2002). Continued threats to staff had their effect, and eventually all agencies withdrew, leaving children unprotected and in an environment professionals feared to visit.

The impact of violence and aggression towards protecting workers has continued, as reported in a number of Serious Case Review reports. Khyra Ishak starved to death in Birmingham in May 2008, in a family characterised by domestic violence. The parents complained of harassment by the social worker, and the health visitor did not sustain visits. The subsequent Serious Case Review report (BASW, 2010) stated that '*agencies had lost sight of the child and focused [on] the impact on themselves as professionals*'. The report blamed the failure of agencies to follow the correct procedures, but did not significantly focus on the barriers to protective agencies doing their work effectively.

The murders of Arthur Labinjo-Hughes and Star Hobson in late 2020 and 2021 respectively, during the Covid-19 pandemic, led to a national outcry, and eventually to a National Review of these cases and the wider child protection system, which was published in 2022 (Gov.uk, 2022). This review was highly detailed and wide-ranging, and covered the complexity of working with non-compliant families and the need for experienced, skilful practitioners working within effective systems. Crucially, however, the report did not clearly identify the impact on workers of working in situations of stress and intimidation and the effect on their decision-making.

There is a disconnect between the conclusions of national reports, the serious case reviews and the lived experience of the workers involved. The reports do not mention the impact of violence and aggression, but the workers see this as a major part of their work in child protection. The impact of violence and aggression on practitioners will be explored further in Chapter 2.

IMPACT ON THE PERFORMANCE OF SOCIAL CARE ORGANISATIONS

The cumulative effect of these factors on practitioners affects the performance of their employing organisations and services as a whole. They affect practice in assessment, analysis, decision-making, care planning and meeting timescales, all of which are evaluated by Ofsted and other audit regimes as part of the inspection process. They also feature strongly in Serious Case Reviews across all partner agencies in child protection. It is clearly in the reputational interests of social care and health organisations to improve practice in safeguarding their staff as part of their overall quality and performance management.

WHAT HAS BEEN DONE TO ADDRESS THIS ISSUE?

Concern about this issue has been raised over many years, including a 1979 National and Local Government Officers' Association (NALGO) report highlighting the effect of aggression on social workers, and a 1988 report by the British Association of Social Workers (BASW) highlighting the risks to staff working with violent and aggressive families.

Following a major campaign by *Community Care* magazine, and the issue of violence and abuse against social workers being raised in Parliament, the government introduced the National Task Force on Violence against Social Care Staff in 2001. This was a major initiative, well resourced, planned and timetabled, which encouraged local authorities to take the messages seriously and implement change to protect their staff. It produced a great deal of material for local authorities and other social care employers including a self-audit tool, sample policies and practice guidance. Despite this, little lasting change was achieved, and the issue was raised again in 2012 in campaigns by *Community Care* and Reconstruct, providing much of the evidence from practice referred to above. The campaign for the safety of social care staff at the national level, including the work of the Task Force, is now being led by Skills for Care (nd).

The issue is still nowhere near being properly addressed or resolved, as is shown by the stories and anecdotes at the beginning of this chapter. Reporting of violent incidents continues to be at a low rate, particularly with regard to verbal abuse and threats. Many incidents are underreported because workers feel, with some justification, that the issue will not be taken seriously by management. It is notable that in agencies which perform well in this area (see Chapter 7), reporting of all incidents, including verbal abuse, is encouraged, and is seen as a part of good practice.

At the time of publishing this update in 2023, there appears to be little active campaigning on the issue of violence against social workers. The UNISON (2022) manifesto for social workers, although valuable, does not specifically address this issue.

IS THE SITUATION GETTING BETTER?

In preparation for this new edition, I held meetings and discussions with managers and staff from a range of social care organisations in adult and children services, to enable me to gain first hand from the experience of practitioners in today's environment. During the course of these interviews, it became apparent that this is still very much a live issue for staff, and one which greatly impacts on their professional and personal life. I interviewed staff and managers from statutory services in different parts of the country, from high performing authorities to those assessed to need improvement, from child protection services to adolescent services and services for the elderly and disabled. Working in situations of intimidation and threat was a common issue, but the ways in which it was addressed varied considerably. Within this there were signs that authorities were taking the issue seriously and investing in resources to protect staff and support them to work effectively for the protection of vulnerable people against this background of intimidation and threat.

A number of themes emerged from this survey as discussed below.

The lived experience of today's social workers

The statistics quoted above give an idea of the prevalence of intimidation and threats against social care and health workers, and highlight the fact that these professions are significantly more at risk than average. But neither these statistics nor the analysis contained in Serious Case Reviews and other reports give an appreciation of the lived experience of the workers concerned, the impact on their personal and family lives and how this affects their ability to work effectively.

Intimidation

Intimidation by service users can be both subtle and explicit. It does not always involve actual violence or specific threats, but the impact on the worker can be pervasive, unsettling and even devastating. It can certainly impact the ability to work effectively to protect vulnerable people.

Examples of intimidation include comments about the worker being racist or homophobic or, in contrast, homophobic or racist abuse from the client. Intimidation can be non specific, and brought about by the presence, for example, of a large male in the room, or a group of people saying nothing, but creating a hostile atmosphere. One worker gave the example of the chair of a child protection conference being intimidated by a large aggressive service user into making a decision not to make a child protection plan, at variance with the views of other participants.

Common examples include clients identifying the cars of workers and following them home, with the implied threat against them personally and their families. Social media sites such as '*I hate social workers*' can be used to name and identify workers and create anxiety.

A large percentage of cases identified were characterised by cases involving domestic violence, which tended to be allocated to the least qualified and least experienced workers, who lack the skills to deal with these situations. Some of the more experienced workers interviewed commented that there appeared to be generally much more verbal abuse and less respect for social workers than ten years previously.

Threats

Workers reported that they had been subjected to realistic threats of violence to their person, their possessions and their families. Examples included threats by brandishing baseball bats and Japanese swords, and one case of a young person threatening to stab the worker with a knife. The use of threats of potential attack by animals such as dogs and snakes is commonly reported. Other workers gave examples of being threatened with being run over or having their car damaged. In some examples these threats were reported to the police, who declined to take action. An example was also given of hostage theory or Stockholm syndrome discussed in Chapter 2, where ongoing threat was part of the relationship with the client.

Violence

Actual experience of violence was reported relatively rarely. However, examples included a client driving a car at the social worker, assault on a social worker by an adolescent care leaver, kidnap, the social worker being bitten by a dog and a gang breaking into a client's home when the worker was present. Despite being relatively rare, experience of actual violence within teams gave credence to the more common threat of violence.

Context

The context of many of these comments was work with children and families subject to assessment, child in need or child protection plans. Some of the work was with care leavers or in the context of youth offending. Since publication of the first edition of this book some new developments affecting work with adolescents have emerged, such as 'county lines' drug trafficking, the trafficking of vulnerable adolescents and contact with gangs in general. Perhaps surprisingly, there were no reports of direct intimidation and violence of workers in these contexts, although there were considerable risks to the young people themselves.

One factor causing risks to young people is that of London gangs moving to economically impoverished parts of the country, and local authorities also placing children and young people in these areas. This can lead to some dangerous scenarios such as placing young people from rival gangs in the same street or social workers visiting young people without the necessary background information. Gangs may not understand the role of the worker and may take this as a threat to their activities.

The impact of social media

One clear development in last ten years has been the rapid growth and use of social media, in particular Facebook and Instagram. This has had its positive impact on social work practice, such as allowing some research on clients prior to visiting, and forming part of assessment information. However, it is also regularly used by service users as part of the intimidation of social workers, for example, the use of name and identify sites, direct abuse of the worker, sharing videos of workers in action (eg during the removal of children) or identifying their cars and homes.

This has led workers to be very wary in the use of their own personal social media, and many have stopped using it altogether. It does seem to be possible for service users to access workers' personal videos and use these as part of an intimidation process.

System and resource issues

System and resource issues can positively or negatively affect practice and the safety of staff. These include factors such as the design of buildings to promote safety and the security of entrances. While remote working, including the use of video-calling for conversations and interviews, can be safer for practitioners, it can also restrict the information needed to conduct the protective task effectively. Evidence of neglect, and the presence of other people in the room, can be hidden.

Initial assessments may have to proceed without vital information about risk. Workers can be sent out 'blind'. Risks associated with domestic violence cases can be underestimated. The absence of essential early help services can result in more families being dealt with by formal child protection interventions which can be more intrusive and provoke stronger reactions.

There is the need to be aware of a balance of power in the relationship between social workers and clients. The role, function and authority of the social worker needs to be clearly understood by families, while also recognising that families must be treated with respect and dignity as part of the process.

Finally, managers and workers throughout the authorities consulted expressed a view that there was a need for better public understanding of the role of social workers and their responsibilities and a more positive public image to be promoted locally and nationally. Currently there is a view that there is no organisation to stand up for social workers, despite campaigns by BASW, Social Work England and UNISON.

These issues will be explored further later in the book in the chapter on effective working.

Consequences

There are a number of significant consequences of the above issues which impact both on workers and on the effective performance of their protective task.

A key issue is the impact of stress on assessment and decision-making. '*The body doesn't want to be there*' said one interviewee. There is an impact on the logical brain and worries that the worker may have missed something. Online working may be less stressful but may not be as effective in protecting the vulnerable.

There remains a view that being subject to low-level verbal abuse and dealing with threats is '*all part of the job*' and that '*some people have it, some people don't*'. However, there is evidence from my discussions that all practitioners suffer from this perceived weakness to some extent, but experience and good team working can help to deal with these issues in a positive way. Due to the culture, it is difficult to get workers to report incidents of verbal abuse and even some more serious intimidation.

Unaddressed, these factors can lead to difficulties in recruitment and retention of staff, and impact on the performance overall of the organisation. The impact includes high cost to the organisation, high levels of sick leave and an overall negative impact on workers and their families as human beings. To quote one first line manager '*We put our lives on the line every day*'.

Workers may have to adopt unacceptable strategies in their personal lives such as going out in disguise, not using their own social media, changing their car or moving house. This can be worse for social work ancillary staff, who may not have the same resources to move out of the area.

Protective factors

The use of protective strategies varied significantly in the authorities consulted, and ranged from basic safety procedures, the use of technology, information sharing and, most effectively, team-based approaches to supervision and planning interventions.

Some basic approaches included visiting in pairs in child protection section 47 cases; this was routine in some authorities but used less in authorities with resource and staffing shortfalls. Other basic approaches include the use of panic codes, GPS trackers and alarms, and laptops equipped with SIM cards to enable emails in emergencies. Lone-working policies cover many of these issues but are not routinely consulted by workers. Some workers had undertaken personal safety training, but this is not accessed consistently.

Information sharing between agencies was seen as critical, particularly with the police, who often have information which could indicate danger. Although information sharing was commonly seen as important, it is not always implemented effectively or recorded on case files. Information from potential clients' social media is now used as part of the assessment process. This information sharing is used in risk assessments which are much more widely used than in the past, but not always consistently.

A key development in promoting both the safety of staff and the ability to work effectively was that of enhanced team working. This was linked to a strategy to reduce remote working based on three days in the office and two working remotely. Proactive approaches that teams can use as part of team and practice development include systemic supervision, trauma-informed practice and training in non-violent resistance for families. These approaches are explored in more detail later in this book.

KEY LEARNING POINTS

Violence against social care and health staff has gone on for many years, and continues at a high level today, affecting the daily lives of professionals.

If not addressed it can put children at risk by reducing the effectiveness of protective services as demonstrated in a number of Serious Case Review reports.

Adverse publicity about the Baby Peter, Star Hobson, and Arthur Labinjo-Hughes cases has reinforced the negative image of child protection work and has increased the potential for assaults on protective workers.

Despite a number of high-profile initiatives and campaigns including a government-sponsored Task Force, the situation is not improving and the problem continues to affect both professionals and the children they work to protect.

Dealing with this issue positively can help improve practice in child protection, and ultimately help achieve improved Ofsted grades for children's safeguarding services.

TAKING IT FURTHER

Brandon, M et al (2009) *Understanding Serious Case Reviews and Their Impact: A Biannual Analysis of Serious Case Reviews 2005–2007*. London: Department for Education.

Brandon, M et al (2020) Complexity and Challenge: A Triennial Analysis of SCRs 2014–2017.

Community Care (2012) Violence in Social Care Graphs. [online] Available at: www.communitycare.co.uk/violence-in-social-care-graphs/ (accessed 6 April 2023).

Department of Health (2001) *A Safer Place – Self Audit Tool for Employers: Combating Violence against Social Care Staff.* London: Department of Health.

Department of Health (2001) *National Task Force on Violence against Social Care Staff.* London: Department of Health. (More detail is provided on this key government document in Chapter 4.)

Health and Safety Executive (HSE) (2009) *Improving Health and Safety Performance in the Health and Social Care Sectors – Next Steps?* HSE Board paper no: HSE/09/84, 23 September.

Lord Laming (2003) *Victoria Climbié Inquiry Report.* London: Department of Health.

Rowett, C (1986) *Violence in Social Work: A Research Study of Violence in the Context of Local Authority Social Work.* Cambridge: University of Cambridge Institute of Criminology.

UNISON (2022) Manifesto for Social Workers 2021. [online] Available at: www.unison.org.uk/content/uploads/2022/03/UNISON-Social-Work-Manifesto-2021.pdf (accessed 6 April 2023).

The physiological and psychological impact of violence and intimidation on professional decision-making

INTRODUCTION

As we have seen in Chapter 1, violence against social workers and health personnel, particularly those involved in child protection and mental health services, runs at a high level in the UK. This chapter explores why this is not only an important issue for the safety of the workers concerned, but also affects their professional judgement and decision-making. This in turn can leave the vulnerable people they care for more at risk.

Actual and threatened violence takes three main forms:

• immediate, unexpected threats or actual violence which 'come out of the blue';

• threats and violence from individuals who have a pattern of aggression in response to certain triggers;

• long-term intimidation and realistic threats of violence within the professional/client relationship.

All have an impact on the ability of the practitioner to function effectively and professionally, and each is explored separately below.

IMMEDIATE, UNEXPECTED THREATS OR AGGRESSION

Immediate, unexpected violence or threats can occur in any professional relationship. This may be impossible to predict due to lack of prior knowledge, or people acting totally out of character. As this is unexpected, the professional may not be prepared to respond appropriately. Later, in Chapter 5, we explore how risks of unexpected behaviour can be addressed.

VIOLENCE AND AGGRESSION IN RESPONSE TO TRIGGERS

Violence and aggression may be part of the repertoire of the service user which occurs occasionally in response to 'triggers'. These triggers may be linked to stress factors such as financial problems, childcare issues, the impact of domestic abuse, actions of other organisations, or a response to the attitude or approach used by the professional involved.

Understanding of personal triggers can be used to help predict the occurrence of violent behaviour with known service users, and safely manage it when it occurs. This is again addressed in Chapter 5 below.

LONG-TERM INTIMIDATION AND REALISTIC THREATS OF VIOLENCE WITHIN THE PROFESSIONAL/CLIENT RELATIONSHIP

Social workers and other professionals are required to maintain long-term contact with families when managing cases of children subject to child protection plans, living with their families. In most cases it is possible for the professional to manage this long-term relationship effectively, and to make progress to secure the long-term well-being of the child concerned. In some cases, however, the relationship is characterised by ongoing and sometimes subtle threats and intimidation by family members. Workers can be controlled by the family by means of intimidation to the detriment of their professional judgement. The response of workers to this threat can have similarities to the response of victims in a hostage situation. This, and the power relationship between professionals and service users, is explored later in this chapter.

It is important to understand the impact of any of these types of threat on the ability of professionals to function effectively.

PHYSIOLOGICAL RESPONSES TO THREATS AND VIOLENCE

When people are subject to physical or emotional threat, an unconscious reaction occurs, preparing the body to stay completely still, run away or fight. This 'freeze, fight or flight' reaction is a deeply inbuilt survival mechanism, common to animals and humans.

A first unconscious response to intense physical threat is to remain totally still in the hope that the aggressor will not notice the potential victim, and leave them alone. This reaction is well captured in the phrase 'like a rabbit frozen in the headlights'. In many situations this can be an appropriate and successful response, helping maintain the safety of the individual.

A second response is flight. Blood will flow away from the periphery and the digestive functions to the major muscle groups, preparing the person to run to get as far away from the violent situation as possible.

A third response is to prepare the body to fight. Similar to the flight response, blood flows to the major muscle groups, including the arms. This prepares the body to fight in self-defence if either of the previous two options is unsuccessful.

In physiological terms, the body's reaction to stress is controlled by the autonomic nervous system. This system controls all the voluntary and involuntary functions of the body, and is divided into the parasympathetic and sympathetic systems. The parasympathetic nervous system (PNS) is dominant in non-stress environments where an individual perceives that he or she is safe. The PNS controls a number of critical survival functions, such as visual acuity, cognitive processing and fine complex motor skill execution.

If the brain perceives an immediate threat to the person's well-being, the sympathetic nervous system (SNS) is activated involuntarily, resulting in an immediate discharge of stress hormones. The SNS drives the activation of the freeze, fight or flight syndrome described above. The release of stress hormones increases arterial pressure and blood flow to large muscle mass, vasoconstriction of minor blood vessels at the end of appendages, changes to eye physiology and cessation of the digestive process. The body is now prepared for flight or to fight.

The downside of this automatic response is that SNS dominance is catastrophic for vision and cognitive processing, as well as complex or fine motor skill performance. Peripheral vision is lost, leading to 'tunnel vision', the individual focusing on the aggressor and being unaware of peripheral activity. The SNS has an even more devastating effect on cognitive processing. SNS activation inhibits higher brain function centres in the cerebral cortex, resulting in a deterioration of the ability to consider and communicate complex thoughts. The ability to think clearly is lost.

The activation of the SNS is automatic and virtually uncontrollable. It is a reflex triggered by perception of a threat. Once initiated, the SNS will dominate all voluntary and involuntary systems until the perceived threat has been eliminated or escaped, performance deteriorates, or the PNS activates to re-establish homoeostasis.

The implication of this automatic response of the body to threat and danger is clear. Professional social workers, health visitors, GPs and other professionals need to be able to think, draw on their professional training and communicate clearly to carry out their role. These very skills are affected by the body's reaction, and may result in the professional being unable to make clear decisions to protect vulnerable children, other service users and themselves.

To perform effectively, practitioners need to feel safe in their working environment or at least feel confident that all threats to their safety have been considered and steps taken to minimise them.

WORKING WITH VIOLENT AND AGGRESSIVE FAMILIES

Research (HMSO, 1995) has shown a strong correlation between child maltreatment and the presence of domestic violence, drug and alcohol abuse and parental mental health issues. The majority of children subject to child protection plans will have one or more of these factors in their family background. It is not surprising therefore that protective workers will often be working with violent families, or families containing violent members, normally males.

In their 1995 report, Farmer and Owen note the strong correlation between domestic violence and physical assault on children, where more than half the children assaulted lived in families where domestic abuse was an issue. Domestic violence is a key precursor to child assault.

The use of drugs and alcohol within families is also strongly linked with child maltreatment, and in the UK the majority of families with children subject to child protection plans have these factors in their background. These factors, and the prevalence of parental mental ill health, are also associated with domestic violence, either as a precipitating factor or as a consequence.

There is a high prevalence of 'absent men' in child protection situations, but men, when they do appear, are often violent and controlling. Mothers in these families can be seen as 'failing to protect' their children. The reality is, however, that they may be subject to continual violence from their men and are psychologically incapable of protecting their children in these circumstances.

Farmer and Owen (1995) also observed that professional attention was often deflected away from the abusive father figure onto the mother.

> *In some cases this deflection was assisted by father figures who made sure they were out during social workers' visits, or even refused to engage in discussions with the worker about the child. In addition, since these father figures were known to be violent men, they could be intimidating to professionals.*
>
> (p 225)

Child protection practice and research focuses on mothers and until recently has tended to ignore the role of significant men in the household. Work with violent and angry men is not part of most social work training and is a significant shortfall. Working with violent men is often seen to be a male preserve, but male workers may be more vulnerable than women as they can excite antagonism in the men they work with. This type of work is often allocated to men due to assumptions that they will be less likely to be intimidated.

Workers tend to avoid men and, as a consequence, *'invest in the mother a child protective power and authority which they hope she will be able to exercise over her male partner'* (O'Hagan, 1997). This can be part of an understandable survival mechanism, but is ultimately a disservice to the vulnerable children they work with.

Violent men have consistently dominated child death inquiry reports produced since 1974 and have been responsible for most of the children's deaths in those reports. Many of the mothers of these children were frequently battered by the men. The threat of violence is real and it is not surprising that it affects practice.

O'Hagan (1997) has also analysed the problem of engaging men in child protection work.

> *Social workers avoid men because of anticipated violence or intimidation. Their fears may be based on actual experience, or the experience of colleagues, or upon an acute awareness of the growing level of violence directed against child protection professionals in particular.*

The presence of violence in families and extended families can result in an intimidating atmosphere both for women in families, and for professionals working in child protection. A history of widespread violence in families where fatal child assault has occurred has been demonstrated in research into child death reports (Reder et al, 1993). This pervasive atmosphere of violence can affect mothers in their protective role, and also professionals who have a duty to fully assess all risks within a family, and who may be deterred by fears of working with violent men.

Lack of training, experience and support in working with aggressive and potentially violent families, and, in particular, aggressive and violent men, can leave children exposed to ongoing danger, even when social workers and other professionals are heavily involved.

JOB CONTEXT

Reder et al (1993) also comment that social workers and health professionals carry out their jobs in a *'complex, fluctuating, emotive and stressful environment. The increased emphasis on procedure driven practice and repeated media coverage makes it easy to understand how violence against child protection workers can be overlooked'*. Much of the pressure on professionals is prompted by child death enquiries and media coverage. Despite this, evidence of violence is often undervalued in child death enquiries and Serious Case Review reports, focusing instead on not following agency procedures and inadequate communication between agencies. The downgrading of the impact of violence and intimidating atmospheres on professional practice, which includes following agency procedures and communicating with other professionals, ignores a major factor in these practice shortfalls.

Working with children, young people and families in the context of abuse, neglect and other adversities places high emotional demands on practitioners, and may well expose them to frightening situations where their safety may be compromised. Responding with empathy to traumatised individuals and disturbing situations can have an impact on workers' personal and professional life (Hendricks, 2012; Figley, 2012; Biggart et al, 2016).

Secondary trauma, also referred to as vicarious trauma, has been defined as *'the stress resulting from helping or wanting to help a traumatised or suffering person'* (Figley, 1995).

Experience of secondary traumatisation in a non-supportive environment can affect workers individually and also undermine team working environments, leading to:

- *feelings of helplessness;*

- *isolation from colleagues;*

- *reduced critical thinking skills;*

- *impaired judgement;*

- *low motivation and poor quality work;*

- *difficulty recognising and monitoring emotions;*

- *increased absences;*

- *high levels of staff turnover.*

(Tullberg et al, 2012; Quinn et al, 2018)

Child protection professionals in the UK from both social care and health organisations are required by their job to maintain contact with children and their families for the duration of the child protection plan. This does not always result in high levels of protection for the children concerned. In a study in the state of Victoria, Australia, Stanley and Goddard (2007) found that the effectiveness of child protection interventions was limited, most children were re-abused and the severity of the case was not reduced. From their data they observed that the only effective protection against physical injury was physical separation from the family. Clearly this does not address the psychological issues of separation from family, but it does call into question the value of current child protection approaches in ensuring physical safety, particularly in the case of working with violent families.

THE IMPORTANCE OF THE PROFESSIONAL RELATIONSHIP

As suggested in government research published in *Messages from Research* (HMSO, 1995), the first precondition for effective social care practice is a sensitive and informed professional/client relationship. As emphasised by two key authors in the development of social care practice, Felix Biestek and Helen Harris Perlman, the casework relationship is central to the intervention process. This, and a sound intellectual approach, is built deeply into the principles of social work as highlighted by Mary Richmond (1917): '*It should be said with emphasis that there can be no good casework without clear thinking.*' This has been a fundamental value in social work training for many years, and still affects the approach of professionals to the task. As will be seen later, this has both positive and negative consequences for the care and protection of children.

Public expectation of social care and health workers in child protection is very high, and failure to protect children leads to press-led denunciation of individual workers. This is another significant stress factor for workers who often also have to deal with aggression from the families with whom they work.

The long-term impact of violence, intimidation and aggression in the job context on individual workers is not recognised by the press, or by many of the professional enquiry reports into child deaths. It is also not sufficiently recognised by employers and managers of child protection workers, who continue to expose inexperienced workers to these pressures without adequate training or support.

In Australian research by Thompson, Murphy and Stradling (1994), it was found that dealing with violent clients and dealing with verbally abusive clients were the tasks that ranked first and second as causes of stress in social work. The more a worker suffers threats of violence, the more they will perceive it as a major stress factor; they do not get used to it.

There is a clear need for serious reappraisal of the support available to social care and health workers to enable them to work effectively in these environments. Currently, some training is provided to staff, but this tends to rely on the initiative of employers, and is not normally taught in qualification training. The training available tends to focus on the management of violence and aggression, but not on managing the long-term psychological impact and its effects on professional decision-making.

Safety checklists can be used to inform risk assessments, including evidence of domestic abuse, previous assaults on social workers, imprisonment for violence and other validated risk factors. An example of such a checklist can be found in Chapter 4.

There is a need to develop a more robust support programme for child protection staff, which includes informed supervision, management oversight of incidents, training that recognises the professional context and utilises additional support when required from partners including the police, and the use of specially trained security personnel. These themes will be developed later in this book.

Social care and health organisations commonly address shortfalls in practice by reorganising management structures. However, some types of reorganisation can result in structures that place most of the day-to-day responsibility on junior frontline workers, who may also have to handle several complex cases at once. Changes in the way services are provided can therefore increase the likelihood of assault, particularly when meeting the requirements of child protection procedures and legislation, when these require intrusive interventions into families' lives.

There is a strong case for ensuring that structural reorganisations recognise the need to fully support and protect staff on the front line, and ensure that they are properly trained and supervised and are able to work with others to ensure their safety and effectiveness in the community. Some recent initiatives with Newly Qualified Social Worker (NQSW) programmes show what is possible when inexperienced workers are properly supported. The issue of what organisations can do to protect staff is explored in more detail in Chapter 4.

THE QUESTION OF POWER

In any relationship between a professional and a service user there is normally an imbalance of power. This is particularly the case when the professional has a statutory responsibility for ensuring the well-being of a child and can use statutory powers to enforce co-operation. In such a relationship the upper hand has traditionally been seen as belonging to the professional.

The power of the professional relies on the application of these statutory powers; but many workers are not prepared to do this, preferring to maintain their relationship by working in partnership with the family. As discussed earlier in this chapter, this balance of power may be affected by the use of violence and intimidation by the family; it may be difficult for an unsupported worker to make appropriate use of their statutory powers to protect the child. This is particularly the case when a hostage-type situation applies, as described in detail below.

Healy (1998) reflects on the use of statutory powers and the way in which workers can be paralysed and prevented from using their power in a productive way. Workers may find it difficult to make negative judgements of the families they work with, and may minimise the extent of assault, abuse and neglect. Burnout can be caused by a sense of powerlessness in workers. These issues are further explored in the Australian Victoria study (see below).

RESEARCH SUMMARY

The Victoria study

This research was carried out in the state of Victoria, Australia, between 1993 and 1997 by Janet Stanley and Chris Goddard of the Child Abuse and Family Violence Research Unit. The researchers examined the protection files of a random sample of 50 children who were, or had been, on a legal protection order, and thus had been subjected to severe assault, abuse or neglect. The study also involved interviews from a random sample of 50 protective workers, of whom 27 were qualified social workers.

Some of the key findings from this research were:

- all of the children in the study remained living with their families during the research period;

- most children experienced further episodes of assault, abuse or neglect following the involvement of protective services;

- the severity of the abuse experienced did not decline following the involvement of protective services.

The authors concluded that

the protection afforded to the more severely abused children was inadequate. These children were not protected from re-abuse. Indeed, many children were re-abused on more than one occasion. Further, the severity of abuse suffered by these children did not appear to be diminished.

The Victoria study also addressed the impact of intimidation and violence on the practice of the workers concerned, their tendency to minimise negative factors within the family, and the subsequent reduction in the protective support offered to children.

HOSTAGE THEORY

Hostage theory can help explain why some children may not be adequately protected in some long-term child protection cases. This theory demonstrates some similarities between the relationship of victims and hostage takers, and that of professionals and the violent families they are required to work with in the longer term. It is based on the Stockholm syndrome described below.

STOCKHOLM SYNDROME

Stockholm syndrome, or capture-bonding, is a psychological phenomenon in which hostages express empathy and sympathy and have positive feelings towards their captors, sometimes to the point of defending them. These feelings are generally considered irrational in light of the danger or risk endured by the victims, who essentially mistake a lack of abuse from their captors for an act of kindness.

Stockholm syndrome is named after the Norrmalmstorg robbery in Stockholm, Sweden in which several bank employees were held hostage in a bank vault from 23 to 28 August 1973. During this episode, the victims became emotionally attached to their captors, rejected assistance from government officials at one point and even defended their captors after they were freed from their six-day ordeal.

Another such example is the famous case of the newspaper heiress Patty Hearst, who was captured by terrorists in 1974 and went on to participate in many of their activities, including bank robberies. This was extensively reported by the press at the time.

The conditions for Stockholm syndrome to exist are where people are denied normal institutional support (from employers, managers and supervisors, and police) and are subjected to prolonged threats to life, bodily integrity and identity. Victims experience powerlessness, helplessness and the effects of the unpredictability of their captor's actions. This results in severe ongoing trauma in an ongoing interaction between victim and terrorist.

Symptoms are profound and long-lasting and may include a range of attitudinal and behavioural changes, anxiety symptoms and depression.

The essential features of Stockholm syndrome include:

- severe ongoing trauma – this creates a hostile, totally dominating environment so that the victim becomes isolated, powerless and helpless, and can be manipulated;

- the length of time and ongoing contact between captor and hostage – a mere threat of physical assault may be all that is necessary to maintain dominance. The syndrome tends not to form where the hostages are physically injured by the captor; there also needs to be some form of positive contact between terrorist and hostage;

- isolation or anomie – the combination of physical and psychological isolation and thus isolation from information;

- the victim employing psychological defence mechanisms, for example denial of the reality of the situation and identification with the aggressor;

- group identification and detachment from the outside world.

IMPACT ON PROTECTIVE WORKERS

Protective workers (including social workers and health workers) are placed in an extraordinarily difficult position as the only workers (with authority to remove children) who are expected regularly to visit the homes of violent people. This regular contact puts professionals (particularly those not strongly supported by their employing organisations) at risk of being subject to a hostage-style relationship.

When workers are explicitly or implicitly threatened with violence on a long-term basis, they may unconsciously act in a hostage-like way and adopt defences for self-preservation and relief from severe stress including as described below.

COPING STRATEGIES

Professionals will need to develop coping strategies in order to remain working with the family. Mikulincer (1994) describes key coping strategies which include:

- problem-solving – using cognitive strategies to overcome obstacles;

- reorganisation – rearranging goals and adopting a more realistic viewpoint;

- reappraisal – attempts to reduce stress by making the mismatch less threatening. This can include reality distortion such as selective attention to positive information, making excuses for bad behaviour, and biasing memory toward positive aspects of the service user's behaviour;

- avoidance – cognitive disengagement with the problem, or physical avoidance such as the protective worker avoiding the abusive male.

Some of these coping strategies are carried out at the expense of task performance. Use of the avoidance coping style is particularly problematic, and can result in cyclical phases of intrusion of the experience and denial, a common pattern in traumatised people. This is a long-term psychological impact, with the worker becoming unable to function, or becoming obsessed with work processes to avoid thinking about these issues.

Figure 2.1 summarises the impact of ongoing threat, trauma and isolation on the worker, who has to learn to cope.

Protection of the child is dependent on the successful resolution of the trauma, and dealing effectively with the situation. The role of colleagues, supervisors and management is critical in reducing worker isolation.

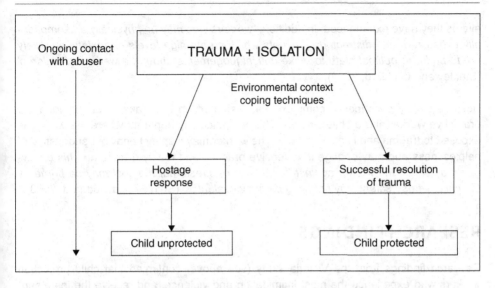

Figure 2.1 The impact of ongoing threat, trauma and isolation on the social worker. From Stanley and Goddard (2009)

DIFFERENCES BETWEEN TERRORIST HOSTAGE AND CHILD PROTECTION SITUATIONS

Despite the similarities described above, there are major differences between terrorist hostage and child protection situations.

- The key difference is that the worker is responsible for the welfare of another person and not just themselves. The lasting impact may be on the child or vulnerable person rather than the worker.

- If the worker is distorting the facts to protect themselves (the hostage effect) they may not use the correct facts on which to base judgements about the safety of the child. If the worker is minimising the violence and risk to themselves, they will also be minimising the violence and risk to the child.

- The terrorist hostage is far more isolated and experiences more dominating threats than would be the case with the child protection worker. However, the worker may be subject to a greater number of traumatising experiences, particularly as they have to interact with a number of people who threaten them, within his or her caseload, and the exposure to traumatic events may last many years.

THE BROADER IMPACT OF HOSTAGE RELATIONSHIPS ON WORK EFFECTIVENESS

Due to the nature of their work and the intimidation to which they may be subjected, protective workers are likely to be particularly vulnerable to reminders of the traumatic events they have experienced. In addition, '*workers who may be physically and emotionally exhausted, and distracted by events which create high levels of anxiety, are likely not to be in an optimal state to make critical judgements about the welfare of children*' (Stanley and Goddard, 2003).

Hostage theory describes a complex relationship which may take place between the protective worker and a child's family. This is particularly apparent where the worker is exposed to trauma and is also isolated. The worker may display behaviour suggestive of helplessness and may engage in defensive practice and reality distortion. '*This behaviour may shield the worker against high levels of stress, but the cost may be borne by the child, whose safety may not be accurately evaluated*' (Stanley and Goddard, 2003).

RESEARCH FINDINGS

Research findings from the Victoria study (see above) confirmed that child protection workers who experience the most intimidation and violence, and receive the least support, sometimes demonstrate hostage-like behaviour. This may in turn contribute to failure to protect some children who have been seriously harmed (Stanley and Goddard, 2003).

In this research, workers routinely reported an under-recall of violence within the families in their current caseload. When this recollection was compared with contemporary notes in the file, this under-recall of violence became evident. To quote one worker, '*The neglect or abuse of a child has become more normal and nothing really shocks me anymore*'. This statement suggests evidence of a distortion of reality and 'burnout'.

WHAT ARE THE IMPLICATIONS FOR PRACTICE AND FOR EMPLOYERS?

Dealing with the long-term impact of aggression, intimidation, violence and hostage-type relationships on professionals, and ensuring that they can work in such circumstances, will require a different approach to supervision, training and support from that which is currently in place.

Child protection agencies in health and social care should formally discuss this issue, look at the evidence, and evaluate practice in their own service to answer the question, 'does this happen here?' If it is found to be an issue, it is likely to be having a significant impact on child protection practice, and will require attention on a single- and multi-agency basis. A clear priority will be to ensure that workers from whichever agency are not subject to long-term intimidation as unsupported practitioners working alone. Multi-agency approaches will be required, and the support of informed supervision. Planned partnership approaches including detailed planning for joint work with families should enable effective work to be done in these situations, and significantly improve child protection practice. A project to undertake local research and the implementation of a joint approach could be a task for the Local Safeguarding Children Board (LSCB).

KEY LEARNING POINTS

The body's freeze, flight or fight autonomic response to threats and danger affects everyone including trained professionals. It is a normal physical reaction, and does not indicate weakness on the part of the individual. As well as the physical response, it negatively affects professional judgement and decision-making.

There is a strong correlation between the families of children subject to child protection plans, and the presence of domestic violence, drug and alcohol misuse and parental mental ill health. It is likely therefore that protective workers will be working with unstable and potentially violent family members.

Men involved with these families are often not seen by the protective worker, but can have a major impact on the family. Reports on child death have found that violent men are responsible for the majority of fatalities in family situations.

The job context for social care and health professionals working to protect children in their own homes requires the establishment of a relationship with the family. The presence of violence and aggression can compromise this relationship.

In such long-term relationships the power balance can shift from the worker to the family, particularly when intimidation and threats of violence are used. Hostage theory can help explain why this happens.

It should be a responsibility of employers to understand these complex factors which reduce the safety of children, and provide more targeted support of their frontline workers.

Supervisors should be trained in these situational issues as part of overall supervision training, and included in reflective practice approaches.

Organisations should clearly record all incidents of violence and aggression, both verbal and physical.

TAKING IT FURTHER

Biestek, F R (1957) *The Casework Relationship*. Chicago: Loyola University Press.

Farmer, E and Owen, M (1995) *Child Protection Practice: Private Risks and Public Remedies. Decision-making, Intervention and Outcome in Child Protection Work*. London: HMSO.

Healy, K (1998) Participation and Child Protection: The Importance of Context. *British Journal of Social Work*, 28(6): 897–914.

HMSO (1995) *Child Protection: Messages from Research*. London: HMSO.

Mikulincer, M (1994) *Human Learned Helplessness: A Coping Perspective*. New York: Plenum Press.

O'Hagan, K (1997) The Problem of Engaging Men in Child Protection Work. *British Journal of Social Work*, 27(1): 25–42.

Perlman, H H (1979) *Relationship, the Heart of Helping People*. Chicago: University of Chicago Press.

Reder, P, Duncan, S and Gray, M (1993) *Beyond Blame: Child Abuse Tragedies Revisited*. London: Routledge.

Richmond, M (1917) *Social Diagnosis*. New York: Russell Sage Foundation.

Stanley, J and Goddard, C (2007) *In the Firing Line: Violence and Power in Child Protection Work*. Chichester: Wiley.

Thompson, N, Murphy, M and Stradling, S (1994) *Dealing with Stress*. Basingstoke: Macmillan.

What practitioners can do to keep themselves safe

INTRODUCTION

This chapter explores proactive steps that practitioners can take to keep themselves safe in situations of potential violence and aggression, including:

1. safety awareness, including in service users' homes, on the street and in the car;
2. risk assessment of situations and service users;
3. planning to minimise risk;
4. teamwork;
5. team safety systems and processes.

SAFETY AWARENESS

In order to fully assess the safety of children living at home, and provide protective support and surveillance, social workers may need to make visits to the homes of their service users or to a meeting point at other locations familiar to them. These may well be located in the less affluent parts of town or the countryside, sometimes in dangerous neighbourhoods with high crime rates. Particular precautions need to be taken when visiting people in these localities, but it makes sense to develop an awareness of potential dangers when visiting people in any community.

There are a number of areas where there are potential dangers for professional staff doing home visits: when travelling, in the community, in the office and in the service user's home. Issues for each area are explored below.

TRAVELLING

Travelling by car, bus and train or on foot is usually safe, but some precautions are sensible and necessary.

In the car

In most areas of the country, the car is the most common form of transport for social care and health workers visiting people in their homes. Travelling by car is normally quite safe, apart from driving hazards. In some neighbourhoods it may be advisable to lock all doors while driving. The main hazards are when parking, and going to and from the car to a visit.

Some important precautions you can take include the following.

- Make sure you know where you are going in advance, using a map, satellite navigation or smartphone.

- Visit during daylight hours if possible.

- If you have to visit at night, try not to park in dark areas – always aim for street-lighted areas.

- Park as close as possible to your destination.

- Park facing the direction you intend to leave.

- Keep keys close at hand when leaving the car.

- Take a loud attack alarm with you and keep it easily accessible.

Public transport

In large cities workers tend to use public transport. In office hours this will normally be very safe, particularly as there are large numbers of fellow travellers. As with cars, how-ever, the main danger may be in walking from the bus stop or station to the service user's address. In this case, as part of your risk assessment you should work out a safe route and avoid potentially dangerous areas.

If you have to visit in the evening or at night make sure you avoid empty bus stations or train platforms unless absolutely necessary. It would be more appropriate to take a taxi, charging this to your employer.

In the street

Wherever possible visit in daylight. If you need to visit in potentially unsafe areas at night, make sure that you fully risk-assess the potential dangers and take necessary precau-tions. If you cannot fully guarantee your safety do not visit at night. If you do visit at night, walk in safe areas that are well lit and where there are lots of people. Carry a personal attack alarm with you and make sure it is accessible. Know where you are going – work out your route in advance. Look confident.

In service users' homes

Most visits to service users in their homes will be completely safe, and you will be made welcome, or at least treated with respect. In some situations, however, particularly in child protection work, you may be viewed with suspicion or hostility. In such circumstances it is sensible to take some basic precautions and be aware of the potential dangers.

Some simple actions you can take are listed below.

- Be respectful, considerate and professional in your manner to your clients. This is not only good practice, but reduces the likelihood of aggressive action.

- Be aware of clothing or jewellery that can be grabbed, eg earrings, scarves, ties, and remove them before entering the premises.

- Be aware of items that can be used as weapons in a service user's home, including kitchen utensils and sports equipment.

- Keep the service user in sight at all times; be aware of their movements and those of other people in the household.

- Have a loud attack alarm ready to use – the distraction of a loud siren noise can help you to safely exit dangerous situations.

- Think about how you dress – not provocative or giving particular messages.

- Do not touch an angry person – it is important to keep your distance to maintain safety.

- If sitting in an easy chair or on a settee, do not sit back into it – it is difficult to get up in an emergency, and easy for an aggressor to keep you there.

- If sitting at a table, sit sideways, so you can leave easily if necessary.

- Make sure your exit is clear.

- When waiting at a door, stand slightly to one side so that people cannot easily rush at you.

- If there is a large dog (or other animal) ask the person to shut it in another room (the excuse of nervousness or allergy can be used).

- Keep your alarm, car keys and mobile phone on you; check that your phone has a signal.

- Use a 'buddy' system so that a colleague always knows where you are and what you are doing.

- If you are working in pairs because of an assessed risk of violence, know what your roles are and be sure to stay together.

- Use an agreed system to report back to the office when concluding any visit out of normal hours.

- Always make sure that your office knows of your whereabouts and your likely time of return. Ensure that there is a procedure within your office for acting promptly should someone not return on schedule – in and out of office hours.

- If you are working from home, and not office based, make sure your colleagues and your supervisor know where you are, and when you are due to return home. Use WhatsApp or another team-based mechanism to keep in contact with your colleagues.

In the office/interview room

- Make sure a colleague knows that you are using the interview room, especially if the interview is with a potentially dangerous client.

- Do not see a client if you are the only person left in the building.

- Keep near the door in order to be able to make an exit.

- Be aware of the location of alarms and how to use them.

- Ensure there is a planned response from colleagues to an alarm being activated and that whoever is on duty knows what to do in the event of an emergency.

In community locations outside the home

Sometimes it is necessary to meet a service user outside their home in community locations. These could be a cafe, community resource, agency office, local park or just walking on the street.

In these locations it remains essential that your supervisor or colleagues know where you are and when you are due to return to the office or home. Risk-assess the location in advance if possible and dynamically when on site. Be aware of any potential dangers, identify your safe exits and consider transport availability. Keep your mobile phones and attack alarms easily available.

RISK ASSESSMENTS

Risk assessments are essential in promoting the safety of professionals who work directly with service users in the community or in their own homes. They can be undertaken by individual staff, in consultation with a colleague, and preferably in discussion with the supervisor or in a team meeting. Risk assessments can be undertaken in respect of individual service users and families. They are also very useful in assessing risk associated with particular situations or activities as part of the professional task.

Risk assessment of service users

Before undertaking a risk assessment it is important to gather as much information as you can about the person concerned. Be sure to check the file for any report of violence against professionals or other people, even for people you have visited before. Be aware of any reports from colleagues and partner agencies which alert to a danger of violence and aggression. Many electronic case record systems have mechanisms for flagging up dangerous clients or situations.

If you have previously visited, discuss with your supervisor any aspects of the service user's home which cause you concern, including dogs, weapons or threatening language.

You can then identify these concerns on the matrix below, and conduct a formal risk assessment, preferably with your supervisor, or if not available, with an experienced colleague.

Area of concern	Likelihood of occurrence	Precautionary action to take
Verbal threats	High	Use a polite but assertive statement that the use of verbal threats will result in the interview being terminated. This will also impact on the assessment and restrict the opportunities for the service user to put forward his or her views. Verbal aggression will be used as evidence in the assessment.
Presence of aggressive dogs and other animals	Medium	Ask client to lock the dog in another room prior to entering the premises.
History of violence against professionals	Low	Fully appraise the history of violence and when it has occurred if known. If the risk is seen as high, visit with a colleague or request assistance from the police.

The questions in the *dangerousness checklist* shown below can be used to help assess the potential for violence and compile risk assessments of individuals:

- Is the person I am dealing with facing high levels of stress?

- Is the person likely to be drunk or on drugs?

- Does the person have a history of violence?

- Does the person have a history of criminal convictions?

- Does the person have a history of psychiatric illness?

- Does the person suffer from a medical condition which may result in a loss of self-control?

- Has the person verbally abused me in the past?

- Has the person threatened me with violence in the past?

- Has the person attacked me in the past?

- Does the person perceive me as a threat to his/her children?

- Does the person think of me as a threat to his/her liberty?

- Does the person have unrealistic expectations of what I can do for him/her?

- Does the person perceive me as wilfully unhelpful?

- Have I felt anxious for my safety with this person before?

- Are there people present who will reward the person for violence?

Risk assessment of activities and situations

Social care and health professionals, particularly those involved in child protection, have to regularly undertake procedures which may cause a hostile response from service users or their families. Examples of this include having to see a child alone as required by a child protection plan. It will be helpful to discuss precautionary action that can be taken, either in a team meeting or in discussion with your supervisor. In some circumstances it may be necessary to pair with another colleague, or request assistance from the police or a security provider.

The table below can be used to summarise these areas of concern, and the action that can be taken to minimise risk to the professional.

Area of concern	Potential risk factors	Mitigating action to take
Having to see child alone as part of a child protection plan	Parent angrily refuses to allow access	• Explain clearly that this is your role. Ask your organisation to provide a written statement of your role and duties in child protection and discuss this with the service user.
Giving unwelcome news	Violent reaction from the service user	• Visit with a colleague if necessary and plan in advance your respective roles. • Prepare the service user for bad news. • Clearly explain the reasons for any decision which has been made. • Clearly explain what options the service user has if they wish to oppose the action, and what support they are entitled to.

CASE EXAMPLE

You are planning to undertake a routine child protection visit alone to see a child, who is subject to a child protection plan. On such visits in the past the mother has normally been present, looking after the child, and her male partner keeps away from the household. This partner has a reputation for violence, and is known to have been verbally aggressive and intimidating with a social worker colleague in the past. You have particularly asked to see the man on this visit to understand his role in the family, and understand that he is likely to be present.

At least a week before this planned visit you should discuss the situation with your supervisor, and undertake risk assessment, both of risks associated with the male partner, and of the situation (having to see the child alone). You should plan in advance with your supervisor the purpose of the visit, and what information is to be obtained. You should also prepare a 'script' outlining what you are going to say to the male partner, and explaining what you want from this discussion. With your supervisor you should assess the extent of any previous violence against professionals, and, if this indicates the potential for violence on this occasion, you should discuss whether it would be necessary to visit with a colleague. If so, you should clearly plan what your separate roles will be. The risk assessment should be formally recorded, and a note of the discussion made in the child's file, together with a follow-up record after the visit. You should report back to your supervisor as soon as possible after the visit itself.

TEAMWORK

As will be explored in Chapter 4, there are many things that employers and their organisations can do to support and protect their staff. Much of this they are required to do to meet legal requirements. To fully protect their staff, organisations need to take the issue and their responsibilities seriously; unfortunately this is not the case with every employer in the social care and health field.

Whether or not the organisation is proactive in protecting staff, there are many things that teams can do to make the job safer.

Firstly the team can ensure that staff safety, and the dangers posed by specific service users and situations, are discussed openly, and preferably within the formal situation of a regular team meeting. A dangerous organisational culture arises when staff are reluctant to discuss this issue for fear of being considered weak or incompetent. In such circumstances the issue remains hidden and, although it may affect many or all staff in a team, anxieties have to be dealt with on an individual basis.

Provided staff safety is an open issue within the team, there are many things a team can do to help support and protect its members.

- Ensure that each office or team has a means of recording the whereabouts of staff at any particular time. This is normally done by means of a whiteboard where staff can record who and where they are visiting, the location and expected return time. If a service user is known to present risks, this should be indicated on the board by means of a * or similar visible device. Such a system can also be electronic, allowing access from smartphones and mobile computers. It is essential that such a system is maintained, and that someone within the team takes responsibility for checking safe return. This would normally be a member of the administrative staff, or a professional practitioner out of hours. The use of 'hot desking' will complicate this process, and electronic forms of reporting back may be necessary. Some firms offer specific smartphone and web-based services to help protect lone workers.

- The coronavirus pandemic, starting in 2020, and the associated imposition of lockdowns, social distancing and general concerns about interpersonal contact have radically changed the way social care practice is conducted. Many practitioners work from home either full time or for two to three days per week, and time spent in the office and interacting with team members can be limited. This isolation of workers can be potentially dangerous and counterproductive to the working of personal safety systems. It is essential that these limitations be addressed on a team and agency basis using technologies such as WhatsApp or mobile phone security apps, and by requiring regular face-to-face team meetings and discussions. Basic security responses such as being aware of the location of workers, when they are due to return home or to the office and mechanisms for reporting that they have done so safely should be in place. This can be a problem for workers operating from home, who may not have anticipated any danger in the planned visit, and who do not activate any safety mechanisms or inform their colleague that they are undertaking such a visit. In such circumstances team members will not be aware of the visit as they would have been when operating in face-to face teams. It is essential that teams and agencies work to ensure that effective team-based safety arrangements are in place to protect their staff while working remotely using any necessary technological supports. They should be agreed on a team-by-team basis as a matter of priority.

- Set up codewords so that staff can alert colleagues by telephone that they are in a position of danger but without having to say so directly. A codeword or code phrase such as 'I will be late back to the office this evening' will confidentially alert colleagues that assistance is required. Clearly, it is essential that all team members are aware of this code phrase, and that a clear course of action has been set out should such a signal be received. This may include visits by colleagues to the service user's address, contacting the police, or other mechanisms agreed by team members and recorded in a local procedure.

- Set up a buddy system with team colleagues.

- Set up contingency arrangements with local police to respond if called to the assistance of a social care or health worker.

- Team meetings should also be used to help risk-assess situations, and plan contingencies. Team meetings could also provide a forum for discussion and practice of self-protection training, including the use of physical breakaway techniques (see Chapter 5).

- Teams should also ensure that records of situations where a worker is at risk are reported regularly to management with a view to formal action being taken. Such records should also be made available to the local union representative.

BUILDING ON TRAINING

Training in staff safety is sometimes provided by employers. It is preferable for such training to be delivered by an organisation familiar with the social care and health professional environment, ethos and working practices. This will help to ensure that the training is based on realistic work situations, the context of the protective role of the worker, and the duty of care to service users.

A sample training programme is provided at Chapter 4.

It is also preferable for the training to be team-based, enabling team members to train together and later to develop systems and processes to keep each other safe. Teams should take the opportunity to regularly review the messages given in training, develop and maintain safety systems, and practise physical disengagement (breakaway) techniques taught on the training.

RESPONSIBILITIES OF STAFF

Practitioners have a responsibility to comply with their organisation's procedures in staff safety. The organisation Skills for Care states that practitioners should familiarise themselves with their organisation's procedures, and implement them. It advises that staff should be prepared:

- when you think there is a risk, discuss your concerns with colleagues and managers;

- report all cases of violence and abuse;

- use local systems to check whether other professionals have flagged concerns;

- gather as much information as possible about people who use services where violence is threatened;

- share information about potentially violent users of services with your colleagues, your manager, other departments and other organisations;

- attend training organised for you.

KEY LEARNING POINTS

Practitioners should be aware of risks to their safety, and learn to take simple precautions to reduce risk in the office, while travelling, in the community and in service users' homes.

Risk assessments are essential to promote safe practice. Risk assessments can apply to individual service users and families, and to common workplace situations and activities.

Risk assessments should be undertaken in conjunction with supervisors, clearly recorded and followed up.

Teamwork is essential to safe practice, and involves team managers and workers devising systems and processes to look after each other.

New working practices have developed post-Covid, including remote working and visiting from home. Teams and agencies should update safe working practices to take these changes into account.

Specific, practice-related training in staff safety should be provided, regularly reviewed, and built upon in team settings.

Staff have responsibilities to comply with employers' policies and attend training.

TAKING IT FURTHER

Braithwaite, R (2001) *Managing Aggression*. London: Routledge (in association with *Community Care*).

Breakwell, G (1989) *Facing Physical Violence*. Leicester: British Psychological Society.

Ross, R G (2007) *Personal Safety and Self Defence*. London: Teach Yourself.

Skills for Care. *Work Smart, Work Safe – Combating Violence against Social Care Staff*. [online] Available at: www.skillsforcare. org.uk.

4 What organisations can do to keep staff safe

WHY SOCIAL CARE AND HEALTH ORGANISATIONS SHOULD KEEP THEIR STAFF SAFE

This chapter explores why employers of social care and health practitioners should work to protect their staff in situations of violence and aggression. It will establish the benefits of doing so for the performance of their service, and to fulfil the duty of care they have to their staff and service users as set out in guidance, codes of practice and legislation.

KEY QUESTIONS FOR EMPLOYERS

The performance of social care and health services depends on the skills, expertise and commitment of their workers, the support and resources provided to them by their employers, and the context in which they work. The role of managers is to ensure that workers can perform effectively; a key part of this is ensuring that they can work safely, particularly in protective services.

Social care employers, their governing bodies and councils should be asked the following questions.

- Do we want to get the best performance from our staff in terms of their delivering high-quality professional work and achieving the aims and targets for our organisation?

- Do we want to show our care of our staff by adequately protecting them and promoting their safety in the course of their work?

- Do we want to achieve and sustain good inspection results?

If the answer to these questions is yes, close attention to promoting staff safety will help to achieve these aims.

This chapter will look at the importance of job design, the requirements of legislation and codes of practice, and the detailed policies and practices organisations can adopt to promote staff safety and effective working practices.

JOB DESIGN

One of the interesting applications of systems theory to organisations is the idea that the success of an individual in a job is more dependent on the support systems around the job – access to information, supervision, training, resources – than it is on the ability, expertise or experience of the person in the post. In fact less than 10 per cent of success is related to the skill of the individual (Seddon, 2003).

Employing organisations need to properly support staff in frontline posts in order to obtain the most value from their investment in employing them. Inspection regimes such as Ofsted are increasingly looking at how staff are supported in order to do their job effectively for the well-being of service users. A key factor in this support will be supervision from trained and experienced supervisors.

An element of this support package should be professional training in working safely to help ensure that practitioners are adequately prepared to conduct their job in challenging circumstances, and to reduce danger to themselves. As explored in Chapter 2, this will also help them to maintain their composure and professional judgement when gathering information and making decisions.

THE DUTY OF CARE FOR EMPLOYERS

Employers have a clear duty under the law to protect staff in the course of their work. The 1974 Health and Safety at Work Act puts a duty on employers to ensure the safety, health and welfare at work of their employees and ensure that their activities do not endanger others. The Management of Health and Safety at Work Regulations 1999 (based on European law) clearly set out what employers are required to do to manage health and safety under the act. The main requirement on employers is to carry out risk assessments of what in the workplace could cause harm to people, and to identify measures to eliminate or significantly reduce the risk of harm.

The trade union UNISON has produced a *Duty of Care Handbook* (nd) which sets out what employees can expect from their employing organisation, and also their duty of care to their service users. This document is supported by the Health and Care Professions Council (HCPC) which regulates professionals in social care and health occupations, including social workers and health professionals.

Under the legislation, health and social care workplaces (which include visits to service users in their own homes or in the community) are required to have risk registers in place to record risks and provide a formal note of the action taken to manage these risks. They should contain information on existing procedures or controls that are in place to mitigate risks and what action should be taken if a risk arises.

Individual members of staff need to have the necessary experience or training to carry out their tasks safely; managers and supervisors should take responsibility for checking that tasks are only delegated to competent, well-equipped individuals.

The Code of Practice for employers of social care workers, developed by the General Social Care Council (GSCC), is at the time of writing held by the Social Care Institute for Excellence (SCIE). This document lays down the responsibilities of employers in the regulation of social care workers. Of specific relevance to staff safety, the code requires employers to have written policies and procedures in place to enable social care workers to meet their Code of Practice standards, including their responsibility for risk assessment and enabling social care workers to work in a safe environment. Employers also have a responsibility to effectively manage and supervise staff to support good practice.

In addition to their duty of care to their employees, social care organisations have to take into account their duty of care to service users, and the standards of government bodies and professional organisations.

Social care organisations are formally inspected against their approach to the care and protection of staff and will need to comply with the requirements of the National Care Standards. Safety of the workforce is a priority of the Training Support Programme. Linking staff safety programmes to Investors in People standards and the requirements of Section 17 of the Crime and Disorder Act would help demonstrate a comprehensive and proactive approach by employers.

KEY RESPONSIBILITIES OF EMPLOYERS

The Code of Practice (GSCC, 2010) advises employers that to carry out their responsibilities for managing risks arising from violence and aggression. This includes:

- making it clear to social workers that bullying, harassment or any form of unjustifiable discrimination is not acceptable and taking action to deal with such behaviour;

- establishing and promoting procedures for social care workers to report dangerous, discriminatory, abusive or exploitative behaviour and practice, and dealing with these reports promptly, effectively and openly;

- making it clear to social workers, service users and carers that violence, threats or abuse to staff are not acceptable and having clear policies and procedures for minimising the risk of violence and managing violent incidents;

- supporting social care workers who experience trauma or violence in their work;

- putting in place and implementing written policies and procedures that promote staff welfare and equal opportunities for workers;

- providing appropriate assistance to social care workers whose work is affected by ill health or dependency on drugs and alcohol, and giving clear guidance about any limits on their work while they are receiving treatment, all while ensuring that the care and safety of service users is your priority.

SUPERVISION

Team managers and supervisors have a critical role in creating a safe working environment for staff. Team managers can help set the culture of the team through positive leadership which promotes staff safety as a key issue. If team managers acknowledge the reality of violence and aggression in the work of their staff, and its impact on their ability to do their job, they can help create an environment where staff feel free to talk about the issue. Once the issue is out in the open it can be addressed positively within the team and in one-to-one supervision.

As has been shown in research (see Chapter 2), the impact of violence, aggression and intimidation can greatly affect workers' capacity to do their job well. Professional supervision is a key place to discuss the prevalence and impact on workers, and to develop strategies to support staff to work effectively. The use of risk assessments should be routinely considered in supervision, in decisions made about whether it is safe to visit a service user at home or interview them in the office and what strategies should be adopted to minimise risk.

The issue of hostage-like relationships should also be addressed in supervision. Supervisors need to be knowledgeable about this issue, and preferably have training in working with resistant families (see Chapter 7), including violent, aggressive and intimidating families and the impact of hostage-style relationships. Given the nature of the effect, practitioners are likely to deny that they are in such a relationship as it would undermine their professional self-regard. They are also unlikely to realise that it is happening, as part of the syndrome is to rationalise their response to service users' intimidation and to minimise the risks that they pose to their children. Supervisors will need to be both knowledgeable and skilled to raise this issue and discuss it positively without generating resistance. This is a key issue in promoting child safety.

Some authorities now use more interactive approaches in supervision including trauma-informed practice and systemic supervision which can provide more understanding of where aggressive behaviour comes from and insights into managing it effectively. Agencies should investigate the use of such techniques.

The checklist below can be used to help supervisors to promote safe practice with their staff.

SUPERVISOR CHECKLIST TO SUPPORT SAFE PRACTICE

- Identify, on each social worker's or health professional's caseload, cases that contain the risk factors of domestic violence, significant drug and alcohol misuse, and parental mental health issues, paying particular attention to those subject to protection plans.

→

- Discuss each identified case with the worker, with reference to the 'dangerousness checklist' on p 36.

- Conduct a formal risk assessment on each identified case, including strategies to address risks identified, including any risk factors that are associated with working from home or online, and other lone-working issues.

- Ensure that each supervision session allows time for reflection on the issues raised in these cases, and in particular to identify whether there are risks to the child, and that progress on the protection plan is robustly monitored and addressed. If visiting in pairs, conduct supervision with both workers. Pay particular attention to the possibility of a hostage-type relationship existing with the worker.

- Ensure that regular, reflective supervision supports direct practice activities (see Department for Education, 2019). Supervisors who show empathy, and are open and understanding, are crucial for reducing the likelihood of practitioners experiencing secondary trauma. Supervisors should be supported to develop skills in containing practitioners' anxiety, enabling a clearer view of what the child and family require and what actions are most likely to produce the best result.

- Review the case record at subsequent supervision sessions to ensure proper recording.

- Discuss the issue of safe practice and risk assessments at scheduled team meetings, at least twice yearly.

PLANNING INTERVENTIONS

Visits, or other forms of contact with families in a child protection context, can be made safer and more effective if they are planned thoroughly in advance. Ruth Pearson (2009) suggests a number of steps that can be taken within such a planning process.

- **Establish what is known about the family before visiting.**
  Establish what is known about the family's history, the form the aggression takes and at whom it is directed. Establish whether there are other risk factors present such as mental health issues and substance misuse. Discuss whether the worker stimulates triggers by keeping people waiting, the threat of loss, discourteous behaviour, lack of alternatives and invasion of territory.

- **Plan the meeting, taking into account the context.**
  Identify the most appropriate place to meet – in the office, at home or at a neutral venue – and be aware of exits, other members of staff, the lone worker policy, access to a phone and other communication devices.
  With a co-worker, ensure that you plan your roles: who will say what and how to manage difficulties. Make sure that you do not trigger unwanted behaviour, eg make sure you arrive on time and are not disrespectful.

- **Agree the purpose of the visit.**
  Establish with your supervisor or colleague the purpose of your visit. Is it for assessment; if so what areas do you want to cover? Is it to see a child alone as part of the child protection plan; if so what might be the difficulties in achieving this and how can they be overcome? How will you deal with any unexpected turn of events – try to predict them and the strategy you will adopt.

Within all this reflect on your own or with your supervisor the family's attitude to your visit or contact. It is not unreasonable for them to resent your intrusion into their lives, which makes it all the more important to treat families with respect while you are obtaining the information and observation that you need. But above all do not forget that your purpose is to support and protect the child, and this should be your main focus of attention. Discuss with your supervisor how you can make sure that you retain this focus.

TEAM WORKING

Promoting staff safety is a team issue. In some teams there has been a refusal to acknowledge the issue, and workers are expected by the team culture to 'toughen up' and deal with issues themselves. This is an inappropriate and potentially dangerous approach, and can lead workers to hide their concerns and internalise their fears, to the detriment of their practice, particularly in child protection. As explored in Chapter 3, everyone, including experienced child protection workers, has a physical and emotional autonomic response to violence, intimidation and stress, and will need to develop mechanisms to deal with it in a healthy way.

A positive team environment, which acknowledges the issue, helps greatly in enabling to manage stress and work-related anxiety. The mutual support of team members is invaluable in developing strategies to keep staff safe while at the same time conducting their work effectively. These strategies are ultimately dependent on good team working, and the development of trust between team members.

The leadership of team managers is essential in promoting such a working environment. Similarly the visible support of senior managers helps to validate this approach, and to ensure consistency between teams in a large service. This senior level support can be made evident to staff by the development and implementation of service-wide policies and procedures, and evident inclusion of the issue on senior management agendas. Involvement of unions in this process reinforces the message to staff that their employers value their staff and are prepared to take positive action to support them.

LONE WORKING AND STAFF SAFETY POLICIES

Employers of social care and health practitioners should establish lone working and staff safety policies to protect their staff in the course of their work. The Code of Practice (GSCC, 2010) recommends that social care organisations should have a written policy statement in relation to violence and abuse against their workers.

Examples of policy statements can be found on the SCIE website (www.scie.org.uk).

EMPLOYER'S SELF-AUDIT

The National Task Force on Violence against Social Care Staff (Department of Health, 2001) developed a self-audit tool to help employers judge whether their organisation's policies for management minimise the risk to workers of violence and abuse, and can support staff if incidents do occur. Although little used today, this document remains valid and a useful framework for employers and is capable of being updated to address risks associated with online working and social media.

It covers the areas outlined below.

Legal responsibilities

> Is your organisation aware of your legal responsibilities in relation to violence and abuse to your workers?

Employers should ensure that they are aware of their responsibilities under health and safety legislation as described above.

Policy

> Does your organisation have a written policy statement in relation to violence and abuse to your workers?

Policies should contain the statement that violence, threats and abuse to workers are unacceptable. The policy should make a clear statement from the organisation which:

- recognises the risk;

- gives a commitment to do something about it;

- says who is responsible for doing what;

- explains what is expected of every care worker;

- supports workers who have been assaulted and abused;

- encourages workers to report incidents.

The policy should be clear about what is meant by violence and abuse. The National Task Force adopted the following definition:

Incidents where persons are abused, threatened or assaulted in circumstances relating to their work, involving an explicit or implicit challenge to their safety, well-being or health.

The policy should cover the organisation's expectations in relation to:

- risk assessment;

- working environment;

- service users;

- social care workers;

- training;

- response to incidents;

- post-incident responses;

- review and audit.

Risk assessment

Has your organisation undertaken an assessment of the risks of violence and aggression facing your workers?

Key issues to be considered in an assessment of risk of violence and aggression against social care and health staff will include:

- environmental risks: in the office, court, home visits, visits to unsafe locations, night visits;

- travel risks: by foot, car, bicycle, bus or taxi;

- situational risks: confronting parents, giving bad news, removal of children;

- risks specific to the service user: known history of violence, use of weapons, drug and alcohol misuse, mental health issues.

Against each risk there should be an assessment of the likelihood of occurrence (low to high).

Action required

> Have you prepared an action plan to deal with the issues identified in the risk assessment?

Preventive and mitigating actions should be considered to reduce the impact. This may include not visiting at night, visiting in pairs or with the assistance of police or security guards, additional surveillance in office-based meetings, and staff training.

A table similar to that below should be completed as a record of the assessment.

Type of risk	Likelihood of occurrence	Preventive action

Staff who work with particularly violent or aggressive people will require specialist training to help them work as safely as possible. This should be considered as part of the training needs assessment, and address the requirements both of frontline workers and of those who manage and supervise them.

Public notices and communications to service users should be used to set the standard of expected behaviour and to highlight actions that will be taken in the event of aggression against staff, which could include withdrawal of service or prosecution.

Response to incidents

Does your policy and procedure make it clear to workers how they should respond to violent and abusive incidents?

Such a policy should clarify expectations of staff, colleagues, supervisors and managers following an incident, and set out procedures for recording the incident, and any necessary actions required. For employers this should include:

- arrangements for debriefing staff and the perpetrator;

- determining actions to be taken in relation to the perpetrator;

- ensuring that colleagues and other agencies are aware as necessary;

- responsibilities for investigation of the incident;

- providing emotional and other support for victims including

  o counselling;

  o access to insurance and compensation;

  o prosecution as appropriate.

The issue of providing effective post-incident support is addressed in detail later in this book.

Audit and review

Does your policy expect and enable managers to regularly check that your arrangements are effective and working?

Management oversight of the frequency, seriousness and impact of violence and aggression against staff is essential in promoting a safe environment throughout the organisation. It is rarely given the priority it deserves.

Such a policy should ensure that a report on violence and aggression at work is considered by the senior management team at six-monthly intervals, and that any necessary organisational response is resourced and implemented. As stated at the beginning of this chapter, the welfare and well-being of staff in a social care organisation is essential for good performance. This issue should be prioritised at the highest level, and include annual reports to governing bodies or councils to promote ownership at political/strategic levels of the organisation.

It would be useful to include the trade unions in this process, or at least provide a report to them, as a demonstration of the organisation's commitment to staff care and protection.

SINGLE- AND MULTI-AGENCY WORKING PRACTICES

As suggested in Chapter 2, a key to effective child protection work in threatening situations is clear planning of the actual face-to-face contact with children and families, whether in an office interview room, partner agency premises or the service user's home.

Dealing with the long-term impact of hostage-type relationships on professionals, and ensuring that they can work effectively in such circumstances, will require an enhanced approach to supervision, training and support to that which is typically in place.

Child and adult protection agencies in health and social care will firstly need to discuss this issue, look at the evidence and evaluate practice in their own service to answer the question 'does this happen here?' If it is found to be an issue, it is likely to be having a significant impact on child protection practice, and will require attention on a single- and multi-agency basis. A clear priority will be to ensure that workers from whichever agency are not subject to long-term intimidation as unsupported practitioners working alone. Multi-agency approaches will be required, and the support of informed supervision. Planned partnership approaches including detailed planning for joint work with families should enable effective work to be done in these situations, and significantly improve child protection practice. A possible approach to this would be the development of cross-agency supervision, similar to that undertaken in Youth Offending Teams.

A project to undertake local research and the implementation of a joint approach should be a priority for the LSCB.

TRAINING IN WORKING SAFELY

Social care and health employers should provide safe working for their staff, particularly those working in child or adult protection, or mental health services, and where they are likely to be in challenging situations with service users in the office or in the community.

This training should be facilitated by a trainer with experience of working in social care and health and should cover:

* identifying the participant's experience of violence, intimidation or aggression to help focus the training on real situations;

- discussing the organisation's policy on staff safety and lone working, and giving a guided tour as to what it contains, and the expectations of staff, supervisors and managers;

- the causes of violent and aggressive behaviour;

- physiological and psychological impact;

- hostage relationships;

- an exploration of the cycle of emotional arousal, which helps to understand the development of a violent situation – see Chapter 5 for details;

- conflict management and de-escalation techniques;

- body language including danger signs and warning signs;

- physical self-protection techniques;

- post-incident responses and actions.

These issues are covered in detail in Chapter 5.

KEY LEARNING POINTS

Promoting safe practice for staff will enable workers to perform better in their protective function, and also improve the performance of the whole service.

Systemic job design will help ensure that staff have the necessary support, resources and training to conduct their work safely and effectively.

Supervision is the key to effective support of staff, including risk management (see supervisor checklist). Approaches including trauma-informed practice and systemic supervision should be considered where appropriate for the needs of the case.

Employers have a statutory duty of care to their staff, and should be compliant with the relevant standards.

Employers should provide appropriate training in staff safety.

Employers should conduct a self-audit to assess their effectiveness in safe working practice (see Department of Health, 2001).

Multi-agency working in hostile situations should be carefully planned and supervised on a joint agency basis.

Ensure that regular, reflective supervision supports direct practice activities (Department for Education, 2019).

The UNISON *Duty of Care Handbook* (nd) aims to empower UNISON members working in health and social care to have a positive influence and be the guardians of safe, effective and high-quality services.

TAKING IT FURTHER

The National Task Force on Violence against Social Care Staff website can be accessed through the Skills for Care website below. This contains a great deal of research and information.

Pearson, R (2009) Working with Hostile or Uncooperative Families. In Hughes, E and Owen, H (eds) *Good Practice in Safeguarding Children*. London: Jessica Kingsley.

Seddon, J (2003) *Freedom from Command and Control: A Better Way to Make Work Work*. Buckingham: Vanguard Consulting Ltd.

SCIE General Social Care Council has a good practice guide and checklists for employers and employees in relation to staff safety, and a number of sample policies which can be downloaded.

5 Keeping safe in an incident

INTRODUCTION

Sometimes, despite all efforts to avoid getting into difficult and dangerous situations, social care and health workers can find themselves in positions where they are threatened with, or actually subjected to, violent and aggressive behaviour. This can be both verbal and physical.

Whatever its form, violence and aggression can have a profound effect on workers and their ability to function professionally. It will impact on the composure of even the most experienced staff, and can affect confidence, self-control and the ability to think and act clearly.

To help manage such threatening situations and to develop a positive response, it is critical for care professionals to understand where such behaviour comes from, what drives it, what the person is trying to achieve by the behaviour and the form it is likely to take.

The aim of this chapter is to help understand more clearly what leads to violence and aggression and to discuss techniques for dealing with incidents, specifically:

* to develop a deeper understanding of why violent or aggressive behaviour occurs and of the factors which influence behaviour;

* to understand the stages of emotional arousal and consider some positive techniques for keeping safe in challenging situations;

* to explore how our own behaviour can help or hinder successful outcomes;

* to recognise the impact of violent and aggressive incidents on the worker and the service user.

THE CAUSES OF VIOLENT AND AGGRESSIVE BEHAVIOUR

Violent and aggressive behaviour can have its roots in trauma experienced in childhood that may persist through adolescence and into adulthood. The approach of trauma-informed practice helps us to understand the ways in which present behaviours and difficulties can be understood in the context of past trauma.

Traumatic experiences can take many forms and can occur as a result of a natural event, as well as being human-caused through accidental or intentional acts.

Trauma is generally categorised into two sub-groups:

- type 1 trauma refers to events which are one time or short-lived occurrences;

- type 2 trauma (also referred to as complex or developmental trauma) comprises chronic traumatic events, which persist over longer periods of time (eg, repeated abuse, neglect, separation and other adverse experiences). This type of trauma generally occurs in the context of relationships (Kinoglu et al, 2017; Herman, 1992).

Adverse Childhood Experiences (known as ACEs) can affect life expectancy and long-term physical and mental health. ACE research organises these experiences into two categories:

1. child maltreatment (eg verbal, physical and sexual abuse, emotional and physical neglect);
2. household adversity (eg mental illness, domestic violence, alcohol abuse, drug abuse, incarceration, parental separation).

These experiences can have severe consequences for children as they become adults and eventually parents. These consequences can include:

- psychological disorders;

- physical conditions that may cause pain or discomfort, or restrict activity;

- developmental disorders;

- use of alcohol;

- use of illicit drugs;

- side effects of prescription drugs;

- genetic predisposition to aggression;

- upbringing and family influences and culture.

These factors are associated with feelings and internal experiences that can fuel violent and aggressive behaviour, including:

- physical pain;

- emotional pain;

- fear;

- anger;

- frustration;

- loss;

- powerlessness;

- grief.

WHAT THE BEHAVIOUR IS TRYING TO ACHIEVE

Aggressive behaviour can be used to achieve an aim or goal. Some people will have learned that challenging behaviour works when trying to get their own way. In most cases it is not directed at the practitioner specifically; it is helpful to realise this and not take the behaviour personally.

FUNCTIONAL BEHAVIOURAL ANALYSIS

It can be useful to analyse the causation of behaviour, particularly by individuals who are well known to the practitioner, using a methodology known as Functional Behavioural Analysis.[1]

This tool examines antecedents, the behaviour and the consequences of behaviour within the ABC acronym:

The 'A' is the *antecedent* and refers to what has come before the incident.

The 'B' is the *behaviour* itself. It is necessary to record a clear and specific picture of the behaviour in order to analyse it.

The 'C' is the *consequence* of the behaviour, what comes after it.

Using this analysis it is possible to identify the aim of the behaviour, and what it is trying to achieve. If the aim is known, more legitimate behaviour can be encouraged to achieve the same goal.

For example, a service user may be violent and aggressive toward you because you have had to report an incident to child protection services or to a child protection conference (*antecedent*). The *behaviour* itself may be shouting, verbal abuse and the threat of physical violence. The *consequence* may be that you leave the house, without the situation being resolved.

In order to take such an approach, and to understand the goal of the behaviour, it is necessary to have as much detail as possible about the antecedent and incident itself, and the actual outcomes. If this is fully recorded it can be discussed with colleagues and supervisors to help you determine appropriate action.

The behaviour demonstrated can be directed at gaining or avoiding attention, accessing or avoiding known consequences, or to avoid or gain sensory stimulation. The matrix below summarises this:

Goal of behaviour	Access	Avoid
Attention		
Tangibles/activities		
Sensory stimulation		

The outcome wanted may be that the practitioner leaves the service user alone. This is not possible in a child protection situation. A better outcome would be for the service user to co-operate to resolve the concerns, and for the case to be closed. In this situation the behaviour you may wish to encourage is a calm dialogue about the issues and what steps you could each take to resolve these.

EXPRESSIONS OF VIOLENCE AND AGGRESSION

The most common expression is anger and loss of control, resulting in violent physical or verbal outbursts. It is rarely planned or deliberate. In social care situations it is understandable why someone may be experiencing strong feelings as a result of the nature of professional involvement, which may be controlling or restricting choice, resulting in a sense of frustration, rejection or isolation.

This can lead to the circular situation described in Figure 5.1: the sense of rejection and isolation can lead to strong negative feelings which in turn may lead to violent and aggressive behaviour. The violent behaviour may then lead to further rejection and isolation, compounding the vicious cycle.

TRAUMA-INFORMED PRACTICE AND STRENGTHS-BASED APPROACHES

Recently developed approaches in child protective work, such as trauma-informed practice, signs of safety and strengthening families, aim to make the issues of concern clearer and more understandable to the service user, thus facilitating positive discussion.

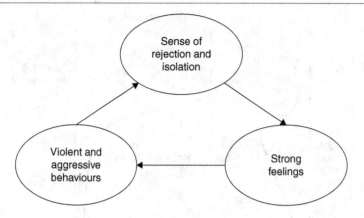

Figure 5.1 The vicious cycle

CRITICAL REFLECTION

Think of an occasion when a service user has acted in an aggressive manner toward you. Use the ABC methodology to analyse the behaviour: what led up to it, what took place in the incident itself, and what was the outcome? Write down everything as thoroughly as possible under the headings of **A**ntecedent, **B**ehaviour and **C**onsequence. Think about what you have recorded and apply your own analysis to understand the reasons for this behaviour, and what the service user wanted from it. You may also find it helpful to discuss this with a colleague or supervisor. You can then try to work out a more appropriate way for you and your service user to achieve the outcomes that you and they want.

THE CYCLE OF EMOTIONAL AROUSAL

Figure 5.2 is based on research into actual incidents of violence and aggression. It describes the process that happens before, during and after an incident. Here, it applies to incidents of violence and aggression, but it can also be applied to other emotional reactions.

Knowledge of the cycle of emotional arousal (Kaplan and Wheeler, 1983) (also known as the assault cycle) is essential to help practitioners understand what is going on in the confusion of an incident, and how to deal with it most appropriately.

Within the cycle there are six interrelated stages, which are outlined below.

Baseline behaviour

Baseline behaviour is our normal behaviour; what people have come to expect of us. Workers in social and health care have the advantage that they normally know people

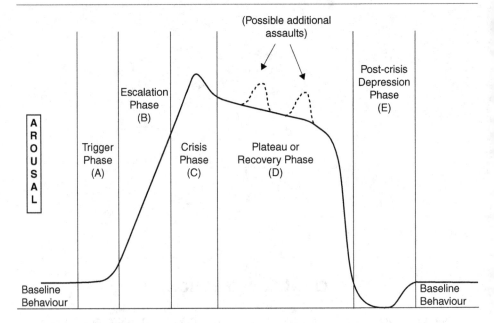

Figure 5.2 Stages of emotional arousal (from Kaplan and Wheeler, 1983)

they work with quite well, and what behaviour to expect from them. People operating within their baseline behaviour should be predictable, and not present surprising or unexpected behaviours.

The trigger phase

All of us, including our service users, have a normal or baseline set of non-aggressive behaviours. However, we all also have triggers which cause us to move away from our baseline behaviours. Triggers vary from individual to individual: typical triggers may be the frustrations experienced at having to queue when in a hurry; people queue-jumping; perceived disrespect from family members or work colleagues; minor injustices; and many other personal examples.

Our service users also have these triggers, and some that may be specific to them or the environment they live in. These may include negative interactions with officialdom or bureaucracy, unexpected changes to schedules and other irritations or frustrations. They may also be a response to illness, pain and discomfort.

These triggers predispose people to react more negatively to outside stimulation, sometimes in an aggressive or violent way.

The escalation phase

In the escalation phase the person's behaviour deviates more and more from baseline. A service user may become overly focused on a particular issue, and become more and more irrational and disturbed. Without intervention the behaviour becomes more extreme and less amenable to diversion.

The crisis phase

As the service user (and the worker) become increasingly physically, emotionally and psychologically aroused, control over aggressive impulses lessens and directly assault-ive behaviour becomes more likely.

At this stage, people are not amenable to negotiation or discussion and their behaviour can become dangerously aggressive. Actual incidents of violence or aggression will nor-mally be short-lived, but there is still the danger of repeated aggressive outbursts follow-ing the initial incident.

The recovery phase

The service user's high state of physical and emotional arousal can remain a threat for up to 90 minutes after the incident, as shown on the chart.

The post-crisis depression stage

After the incident has fully passed, the person's mood can drop below their baseline. Mental and physical exhaustion is common and the service user may become tearful, remorseful, guilty, ashamed, distraught or despairing.

Build-up through the trigger, escalation and crisis phases can vary: with some individuals it will be a very short-duration process, and with others a much more gradual build-up. The plateau or recovery phase takes up to 90 minutes, during which time great care should continue to be exercised.

It is important to remember that victims and any witnesses will follow a similar path. The professional worker will also be affected by the incident, and follow a similar emotional arousal path to that of the service user.

Remember, understanding challenging behaviour will help you deal with it more effectively.

THE PHYSIOLOGY OF STRESS: WHAT IS ACTUALLY HAPPENING TO THE BODY WHEN IT IS UNDER STRESS?

Our body's reaction to stress is rooted in our ancestry. The freeze, fight or flight autonomic reaction to stress has been discussed in detail in Chapter 2. A summary of the key physical responses follows below.

In response to the threat of violence and aggression:

- the muscles become tense;

- the adrenal glands release to get the defence reaction going and sustain it;

- the heart beats faster, blood pressure rises, the major blood vessels dilate and more blood is therefore sent to vital organs, eg the muscles needed to run away or to fight;

- faster breathing increases the oxygen supply to produce energy and eliminate the waste carbon dioxide;

- the liver releases glycogen (stored sugar) into the blood supply, raising blood glucose for energy;

- stored fats are released, again for use as energy by the muscles;

- the skin sweats to keep the body cool;

- the eye – pupils dilate to improve our sideways vision to find a way of escape;

- the digestive system slows down and almost stops temporarily as the blood is diverted to priority organs, eg muscles. The food stays longer in the stomach, the bowel slows down and the bowel sphincters close;

- the bladder sphincters close.

There are many other physical changes, but these are the most significant.

This reflex was a life saver for our prehistoric ancestors who had to 'fight' or 'flee' regularly to save their lives. Occasionally, it is useful for us if we need to respond very rapidly on a physical level to a threat: for example, if we are charged by a bull while sitting in a field, a surge of energy may help us reach the gate in time.

This is an emergency reaction for use in the short term only, followed by a time for 'winding down', after the chase or the fight, during which the affected organs in the body can return to normal.

This physiological response has the downside of shutting down higher intellectual functions, making the ability to think clearly virtually impossible.

Problems develop when the reaction is sustained for longer periods of time, as happens too frequently in the present day. The perceived 'threats' in modern society are less likely to take the form of physical attacks on us. Rather they come from psychological pressures resulting from the many different and often conflicting demands made on us, as we attempt to fulfil expectations laid on us in our various roles as workers, parents, partners, colleagues, friends, etc. When experiencing 'distress', the body systems are put out of balance and then remain in this state, resulting all too often in ill health.

The irony is that what was intended as a life saving reflex is now one of the major causes of serious illness in our society.

BODY LANGUAGE AND NON-VERBAL COMMUNICATION

It is helpful for workers to understand that both their own and their service user's non-verbal signals are the primary means of communicating, particularly when situations are emotionally charged. As summarised in Figure 5.3, 55 per cent of the impact of communication is through non-verbal means, and only 7 per cent through the spoken word.

The study of body language is a complex area, but the basic ideas are simple. Firstly, body language is a truthful language; it is largely automatic, is generated by basic and deep responses to situations and is difficult to control. This is, however, a matter of degree. It is almost impossible to contain the major responses of your body: for example if you wish to leave a room urgently, your feet tend to turn in that direction before you are

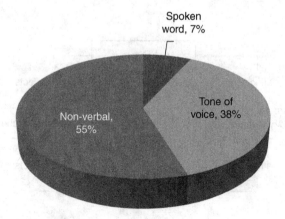

Figure 5.3 Non-verbal communication

able to do so. People will keep a distance from each other dependent on how comfortable they feel. Major movements of the arms and upper body demonstrate strong emotions, from love and affection to fear and hatred. These include both welcoming and warding-off gestures, as well as indications of increasing excitement or distress.

Facial expressions are the easiest to control, and can be used to give the wrong impression. A good example of this is a false smile, which can be detected by a trained observer.

When trying to read a person's body language, particularly in a stressful situation, it is better to focus on the major body movements initially, rather than relying on facial expression.

HOW OUR OWN BEHAVIOUR CAN AFFECT OUTCOMES

When dealing with violent or aggressive behaviour it is important to realise that the only behaviour you can really control is your own. How you behave toward your service user both at normal times and at a point of crisis can significantly affect what happens.

A useful model to help understand this is Batari's box (see Figure 5.4).

BATARI'S BOX

As human beings we mirror each other's behaviour: the other person's behaviour affects our own attitudes, which in turn affect our behaviour. This is a circular process which can take the form of a positive spiral in which our behaviour and attitudes towards each other improve, or a negative spiral (vicious cycle) in which our behaviour and attitudes continue to deteriorate, increasing the possibility of aggression.

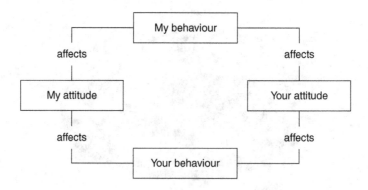

Figure 5.4 Batari's box

In managing aggression remember the importance of *self-presentation*, otherwise *self-preservation* may become your priority. It is crucial that professionals avoid mirroring aggressive behaviour and remain, or at least appear, calm. Modelling and expressing calm behaviour can have the opposite, positive de-escalating effect – but this can be easier said than done.

In practice, the following advice has proved useful to help professionals to remain calm.

*   Keep breathing – take deep breaths in and breathe slowly out.

*   Drop your shoulders and use open, non-aggressive hand signals.

*   Stand at a slight angle and maintain your distance.

*   Do not show that you are afraid – even if you are. Tell yourself that you can deal with this.

*   Request the behaviour you want or want to stop, eg 'Please stop shouting at me'.

*   Do not smile – it may be seen as patronising or as meaning that you think the person's problems/feelings are funny.

Avoid sending any aggressive signals. If you appear aggressive you will be more likely to be attacked.

RECOGNISING AND USING BODY LANGUAGE FOR PERSONAL SAFETY: DISTINGUISHING BETWEEN WARNING AND DANGER SIGNS

It is essential for social care and health professionals to be able to distinguish between body language signs which warn of impending aggression, and danger signs which show that it is no longer safe to be in the presence of the individual displaying them. Being able to distinguish between the two enables a practitioner to decide whether to intervene to try to de-escalate the behaviour, or to leave the scene to keep themselves safe.

Warning signs

Generally aggressors who are aroused to fight do not launch into an assault, for fear of injury. They begin by using attack gestures. By learning to identify these signals you give yourself a significant advantage in being able to manage the situation and keep yourself safe.

Warning signs have been identified through observation of incidents of violence and aggression and include:

- direct prolonged eye contact with a clear aggressive intent;

- deepening of facial colour, noticeable even in those with darker skins;

- the head being inclined backwards to maximise height;

- the person standing as tall as possible to maximise height;

- kicking the ground with the ball of the foot;

- the person making large hand movements close to you;

- the person's breathing rate accelerating noticeably.

Additionally the person may exhibit personal identification; they indicate that you are the problem and as a consequence begin directing the aggression towards you.

Practitioners should be aware that when they identify these signals, the person is becoming distressed or aroused to the point where violence may occur. At this stage it is still possible, however, to use distraction and de-escalation techniques (see later in this chapter), as the service user is still able to think and process information.

Danger signs

Danger signs are much more serious than warning signs, and *must not be ignored*. The person will begin to lose control both mentally and physically. They become unable to listen or process information, and will not respond to attempts at calming. Social care and health workers need to understand and recognise the signs, as they indicate a strong possibility of attack.

Danger signs include:

- fists clench and unclench;

- the person's facial colour pales as adrenaline causes blood to be withdrawn from the extremities and into the major muscles of the body;

- lips tighten over teeth: this is difficult to describe but in fact is a natural gumshield to protect teeth from damage – loss of teeth could be life-threatening in earlier times;

- eyebrows drop to protect the eyes;

- hands rise above waist, indicating a readiness to strike;

- shoulders tense;

- stance changes from square to sideways: this has been identified from police videos of incidents. A side-on stance is a natural reaction to protect the major organs of the body from harm;

- person breaks stare and focuses on the intended target area;

- if the target is out of reach, the final sign of attack will be a lowering of their entire body before moving forward.

NB: Some people can hide warning signs but very few people can cover up danger signs.

Recognising danger signs is essential. The time to make a space between you and the person, or to make your exit, is when there is a combination of two or three of these signals.

WHAT CAN YOU DO TO PROTECT YOURSELF AND MANAGE SITUATIONS OF AGGRESSION AND VIOLENCE?

Conflict management techniques

It is important to understand what conflict management techniques are useful at what stage in the emotional arousal cycle.

The following conflict management techniques are appropriate in the early stages of emotional arousal.

Apologise

... if you are in the wrong, or have contributed to or misunderstood the situation. If you do apologise make sure that you show that you mean it. An obviously half-hearted apology can make things worse.

Apologies are a very powerful tool in resolving violent and aggressive situations. It is helpful to reflect how an apology can affect you personally. For example, if someone has been unintentionally disrespectful to you, or has caused you unnecessary inconvenience, an apology can quickly relieve any feelings of resentment you may have. This is an essential element in customer relations in shops and services, and can have a powerful impact in the social care or health environments.

Listen

Don't be too quick to jump in with reasons, justifications and explanations. It is important to let people finish their story and show that you are listening to them; they will calm down as they get it off their chest.

Understand

... and show that you do. Check out as necessary and acknowledge their feelings, but remember that it is usually unhelpful, and can be provocative to say that you 'know how they feel'.

Give information

... as fully and honestly as possible. If you do not know, say so.

Remove the audience

People who are demonstrating aggressive or violent behaviour often play to any audience that may be present. If you or your colleagues are able to remove this audience it will help to more quickly resolve the situation.

Give space

It is important to realise that the audience could be yourself if you have become the focus of the person's escalating anger/fear, etc. By withdrawing you may give the person the opportunity to regain some control.

Stay calm

... on the outside at least. You can panic later. Be aware of your own body language; use open, non-threatening gestures.

Get them to sit down

… and then sit down yourself so you don't intimidate them. Do not sit in the hope that they do; you will be very vulnerable.

A word about humour

Humour used well can be very effective in de-escalating a situation. The danger, however, is that the person may think you are laughing at them, and will become more aroused.

De-escalation techniques

De-escalation techniques can be used to defuse situations in the escalation phase, when warning signs are evident. They will not be effective when danger signs appear. They include:

- appropriate use of humour – but only if you know the person very well, and know how they are likely to react;

- talking calmly to the person concerned, inviting and exploring their point of view;

- silence when appropriate – this is non-threatening and gives the person space to think;

- giving choices about what can be done to resolve the situation, speaking in a calm voice;

- warning of consequences if the behaviour continues. Try to explain consequences logically and calmly, and not use them as a threat;

- calling people by their name to establish rapport and identification;

- using 'I' and your own name to help build trust;

- reminding them of your relationship and of your past history of working together;

- distraction/diversion – changing the subject to something that you know the service user is interested in;

- being assertive and being clear what you want from the service user, eg asking them to stop shouting as it makes you uncomfortable and gets in the way of being able to resolve the situation;

- ignoring the behaviour – this is only helpful in certain circumstances. Normally it is better to intervene as early as possible to discourage the behaviour. Ignoring initial behaviour can lead to more extreme behaviour.

RESPONDING TO AGGRESSIVE AND VIOLENT BEHAVIOUR ASSERTIVELY

In working with families Ruth Pearson (2010) advocates an *assertive, confident approach* (Koprowska, 2020), and *soft, mindful and judicious use of power*. This includes:

- being aware of one's power and the normalcy of client fear, defensiveness and anger;

- responding to client negativity with understanding and support instead of counter-hostility and coercion;

- listening to and empathising with the client's story;

- pointing out strengths and conveying respect;

- following through on one's responsibilities and promises.

McBride (1998) describes assertive social workers as having appropriate behaviour that is halfway between aggressive and passive. They feel confident about themselves, and respect themselves and others equally. They have clear goals and outcomes in mind and are able to say they don't know or they don't understand to get clarity of communication from the other person.

Communication of personal opinions, needs and boundaries is the behavioural middle ground, lying between ineffective passive and aggressive responses, and can be very effective in responding to violent and aggressive behaviour, maintaining personal integrity while not exacerbating the situation. This approach is guided by a number of principles.

- Assertiveness involves making your rights and feelings a priority while not infringing the rights of others.

- Assertiveness involves working towards positive outcomes; it is not about winning and losing.

- Assertiveness involves negotiation, co-operation, communication and trust.

- Assertiveness is not about getting your own way.

EFFECTIVE RESOLUTION VERSUS WINNING

There is considerable anecdotal and research evidence (Millham and Bullock, 1976) to suggest that in many professional social care situations, violent incidents develop because workers fear losing 'face' or control. As a consequence, they respond confrontationally to low-level challenging behaviour, often escalating the situation. In social care and health situations it is important to focus on the objective of defusing and de-escalating aggression, rather than on winning the immediate argument, or demonstrating your power and control. Putting across the professional view can take place after the incident has ceased, when people are more receptive to discussion and more likely to take on board the need for change.

The ability to make the distinction between *de-escalating* and *winning* is crucial in effectively managing behaviour.

Self-protection

If the worst comes to the worst and the practitioner is seriously threatened with a potential assault, there are a number of physical defensive actions which can be taken to help keep them safe. The fundamental safety precaution is keeping a safe distance.

The importance of keeping safe distance

People are very aware of the importance of personal space. There are three main dimensions of personal space.

1. *Social space or distance*: this is the space between individuals in which people feel comfortable talking or interacting in a social setting. Others do not enter your personal space, and you do not enter theirs. In normal circumstances this is about an arm's length apart.
2. *Personal space*: this is an individual's own space, which they feel uncomfortable about others entering. Exceptions to this are intimate relationships, and some brief social interactions such as hugs and social kisses.
3. *Safe distance*: this is the distance maintained between individuals where it is difficult for an aggressor to enter an individual's personal space for the purpose of assault. It enables a person to have sufficient time to react if an attempted assault is started. It also protects against some behaviours experienced in the care setting such as clothing grabs or hair pulls which may not be aggressive in intent but can be painful or difficult to deal with.

Safe distance would normally be at least two arms' lengths.

Being aware of and maintaining a safe distance in potentially violent or aggressive situations is extremely important for social care and health professionals. It greatly minimises the possibility of assault or harm. This space can be maintained by using strong non-verbal gestures, such as a 'stop' hand signal, and moving away to maintain distance from an aggressor.

Basic breakaway training

As discussed above, the most important technique in self-protection is maintenance of distance. However, if an assault is actually initiated, there are some simple techniques for disengagement (breakaway) which are beyond the scope of this book but can be learned on professional training courses. These may include releases from and defences against common assaults such as:

- wrist grabs;

- clothing grabs;

- hair pulls;

- strangulation;

- crushing attacks;

- kicks and blows.

It is essential that training on these issues takes place with qualified trainers and is not practised casually. Techniques taught should be easily learned and remembered, not overly complex or reliant on physical strength, size or fitness.

What techniques and approaches to use when

It is important for practitioners to recognise what techniques and approaches can be used at different stages of the emotional arousal cycle. Diffusion, conflict management and de-escalation techniques, which can be used effectively at the trigger or escalation phase, will not be effective at the crisis stage and are potentially dangerous. The following table gives advice on how to respond.

Emotional arousal cycle stage	Appropriate response
Baseline	Get to understand the baseline behaviour of your service user. Try to avoid triggers. Know when the person is moving away from baseline behaviour. Share this information with your colleagues, and record in a risk assessment profile
Trigger	Use conflict management and defusion techniques
Escalation	Use de-escalation techniques
Crisis	Don't intervene Don't get too close, and if possible exit to a safe distance

Emotional arousal cycle stage	Appropriate response
Assault	Maintain or create distance
	Use basic self-protection techniques and disengagement
	Use teamwork if a physical intervention (restraint) is required, using trained techniques
Recovery	Give space to the service user
	Don't get too close as there is a danger of repeated incidents. It is inadvisable to put your arm around a person who is still within the recovery phase
Post-incident depression	Give the service user or member of staff support and understanding
	Work with the service user to plan the way forward
	NB: It is not helpful at this stage to review the incident in detail. See Chapter 6 on post-incident responses

Post-crisis reactions

Feelings in the aftermath of violence

People's reactions to violence are unpredictable: many feelings can be experienced simultaneously. They are seldom linear or compartmentalised. Some of the different reactions are shown in Figure 5.5.

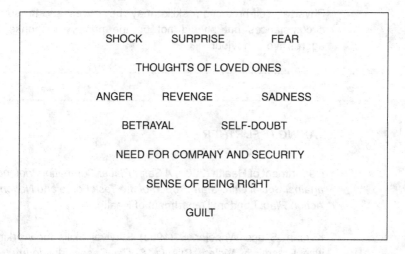

SHOCK   SURPRISE   FEAR

THOUGHTS OF LOVED ONES

ANGER   REVENGE   SADNESS

BETRAYAL   SELF-DOUBT

NEED FOR COMPANY AND SECURITY

SENSE OF BEING RIGHT

GUILT

Figure 5.5 Reactions to violence (Leadbetter and Trewartha, 1996)

Each of these reactions requires a different response from individuals giving post-incident support. It is normally helpful to give people who have been involved in violent situations the opportunity to express their feelings in their own way before offering comment.

KEY LEARNING POINTS

It is important to understand the causes of behaviour and where it is coming from.

Trauma-informed practice and strengths-based approaches such as strengthening families and signs of safety can help understand the experiences which drive aggressive behaviour.

Functional Behavioural Analysis and the use of the ABC methodology (antecedent, behaviour, consequence) is a useful tool to understand the behaviour itself.

Knowledge of the cycle of emotional arousal helps social workers to understand when it is and is not safe to intervene.

Non-verbal communication gives clues to the thoughts underlying behaviour. It is important to understand warning and danger signs of impending aggression.

Assertive responses to potentially aggressive behaviour provide the best outcomes for worker and service user.

Physical self-protection skills may be necessary in some circumstances but should not be the primary response to aggressive behaviour.

TAKING IT FURTHER

Department of Health (2000) *A Safer Place: Combating Violence against Social Care Staff. Report of the Task Force and National Action Plan*. London: Department of Health.

Kaplan, S and Wheeler, E (1983) Survival Skills for Working with Potentially Violent Clients. Social Casework. *Journal of Contemporary Social Work*, 64(6): 339–46.

Leadbetter, D and Trewartha, R (1996) *Handling Violence and Aggression at Work*. Lyme Regis: Russell House Publishing.

McBride, P (1998) *The Assertive Social Worker*. Aldershot: Arena.

Mehrabian, A (1981) *Silent Messages: Implicit Communication of Emotions and Attitudes*. Belmont, CA: Wadsworth.

Millham, S and Bullock, R (1976) *New Residential Approaches*. Proceedings of 1976 conference, Association for the Psychiatric Study of Adolescence.

Navarro, J and Karlins, M (2008) *What Every Body Is Saying*. New York: Harper.

Pearson, R (2010) *Getting through the Door: Working with Overtly Uncooperative Clients to Move Past Barriers*. Presentation to Community Care Conference, November.

Wilkinson, J (2018) Developing and Leading Trauma-Informed Practice. Research in Practice Leaders' Briefing. [online] Available at: www.researchinpractice.org.uk/children/publications/2018/august/developing-and-leading-trauma-informed-practice-leaders-briefing-2018/ (accessed 31 May 2023).

Dale Carnegie's classic book *How to Win Friends and Influence People* also gives some useful techniques for managing difficult situations respectfully and effectively.

Website:

HSE (Health and Safety Executive) (nd) Employers' Responsibilities. Gov.uk. [online] Available at: www.hse.gov.uk/workers/employers.htm (accessed 12 June 2023).

NOTE

1 Functional analysis in behavioural psychology is the application of the laws of operant conditioning to establish the relationship between stimuli and response, based on the work of BF Skinner et al (Morris et al, 2005). For more information see the *Journal of Applied Behavior Analysis*.

6 **Post-incident responses**

INTRODUCTION

Incidents of violence and aggression, however well managed, are not without their consequences which affect everyone involved. This will include the victim, witnesses or colleagues, managers and the perpetrator. The impact will include physiological, emotional and behavioural consequences. Managing the aftermath of such instances is almost as important as managing the incident itself, to minimise long-term damage.

The following exercise can be used by you and your team colleagues to consider the impact of a violent or aggressive incident. NB: *Be careful when you use this exercise* as it can bring back strong feelings and memories of a distressing incident. It is better to do this exercise when you have access to someone you can talk to afterwards, or do it jointly with a trusted colleague.

REFLECTIVE EXERCISE

Think of a situation you have been in which involved intimidation, verbal aggression or assault. If you have not been in such a situation yourself, focus on an incident that happened to a colleague. When you have brought this situation to mind, reflect on the following.

- What happened before the incident?

  - Was it something that had happened before, or did it come completely out of the blue?

  - Was there any way you could have predicted it happening?

  - Was there a response to a trigger that started the incident?

  - Was the aggression perpetrated by one person or a number of people?

- What happened during the incident itself?

  - Describe to yourself or a colleague what actually happened. Include both physical and verbal aggression.

- ○ Think about how you felt during the incident (eg fear, becoming immobile, wanting to run away, wanting to fight back).

- ○ Were you in control of your actions?

- ○ Were you able to think clearly?

- What happened immediately after the incident?

  - ○ Describe any physiological reactions (eg feeling sick, shaking).

  - ○ Describe any emotional reactions (eg anger, fear).

  - ○ Describe any behavioural reactions (eg started smoking, reluctant to go out alone).

  - ○ Any other feelings or reactions.

  - ○ What did your colleagues do to help you?

- What happened in the hours or days after the incident?

  - ○ What did your colleagues do to help you?

  - ○ What did your manager do?

  - ○ What reports did you have to write? Did you feel able to do this clearly?

  - ○ Did you have further contact with the perpetrator?

  - ○ What happened to the perpetrator?

  - ○ Did you make any changes to the way you work?

  - ○ Did your organisation make changes to procedures or policies?

Now think about anything that you would like to have done differently in the above situation.

- What would you have liked your colleagues or managers to do differently?

THE ROLE OF COLLEAGUES

As a team, consider what your role should be as colleagues of someone who has been subject to verbal aggression, intimidation or assault. Think about and discuss the following questions.

- What support should you give your colleague during the incident itself if you are present?

- What support should you give immediately after the incident?

- What support should you give after the situation has calmed down, and in the medium term?

- What support should you give in the longer term?

- What changes should you make to working as a team?

When considering these issues, bear in mind the effects summarised in the 'cycle of emotional arousal'.

THE ROLE OF MANAGERS AND SUPERVISORS

If you are a manager or supervisor consider what actions you should take to support your team member during and after an incident. If you are not a manager consider what actions you think your manager should take to help support you as a victim.

- What action should you take immediately after the incident?

- What is the most appropriate time to debrief your member of staff, and ask for a report of the incident?

- What should you be aware of when debriefing, and requiring a report?

- What action can you take to help prevent such an incident occurring again?

- What else can you do to help and support your team member?

ACTIONS IN RESPECT OF THE PERPETRATOR

As a practitioner, team member or manager consider what action should be taken in respect of the perpetrator.

- What support might the perpetrator need after the incident?

- What discussions should be held with the perpetrator?

- What sort of action with the perpetrator may be necessary to help prevent the situation recurring?

- What sort of legal intervention may be required?

- What report would you need to make to your managers?

Consider your responses to the above questions, and compare them to the responsibilities of employers as set out below.

DUTY OF CARE TO STAFF

Employers have a duty of care to both service users and their staff as set out in the GSCC Code of Practice (2010). It is essential that duties are taken seriously and addressed thoroughly. The UNISON *Duty of Care Handbook* (nd) sets out the responsibilities of employers under the legislation with reference to good practice guidance. The key points are summarised below.

Support from colleagues

A first duty in any organisation is for colleagues, supervisors and managers to provide support as soon as possible after the incident. Support should be distinguished from debriefing. Support is looking after staff; debriefing is providing information on the incident and is important for the organisation and improving future practice. It is important that each is done, but attempting to do both at the same time can result in neither being addressed satisfactorily. Doing the right thing but at the wrong time can lead to as much harm as, if not more harm than, failing to act.

Support from managers

In supporting colleagues who have experienced an incident of violence or aggression, colleagues and managers should:

- immediately attend to any injuries, involving first-aid trained staff or referral to a hospital or doctor as required;

- take the situation seriously;

- ensure that it can be discussed in private;

- allow and acknowledge personal feelings in relation to the service user;

- be prepared for unexpected feelings – people react differently to violent and aggressive situations, and they may link powerfully with feelings from the past which may be unknown to colleagues;

- pre-agree the level and manner of feedback to the team;

- consider additional support that may be required, eg from occupational health for stress at work.

Debriefing

Debriefing should only take place when the member of staff has calmed down and is able to talk rationally. This is likely to be at least 90 minutes after the episode. When debriefing, managers and supervisors should:

- ensure the accurate recording of the incident using the organisation's incident forms;

- be specific in recording – avoid generalisations;

- complete records as soon as possible, but always when the member of staff is ready to report;

- ensure managers are informed of the incident in accordance with local procedures;

- inform the health and safety officer in accordance with local procedures;

- complete accident forms if necessary.

Management responses

Employers, through their managers, should provide debriefing sessions both for the worker and for the perpetrator. It is extremely important to do this after any significant or cumulative incident, as it gives a strong message of support to the professional and ensures that perpetrators are aware that violence and abuse is taken very seriously on every occasion.

Managers should determine actions to be taken in relation to the perpetrator. This may include changing visiting arrangements, not conducting home visits or visiting in pairs, and must include the possibility of withdrawing service. This will not be possible in child protection situations, and other arrangements will need to be made to ensure the safety and security of professional staff. This may appear to be more intrusive from the service user's perspective.

Managers should ensure that colleagues and other agencies who are in contact with the perpetrator are aware of the incident, to enable them to take precautionary action.

Managers should ensure that the incident is properly investigated and recorded on the service user file, and on the health and safety record.

Managers should also ensure that the correct level of emotional support is provided for victims.

Employers should be clear about what support is available to workers in relation to:

* counselling;

* insurance and compensation;

* prosecution.

Employers should also have a process in place for audit and review, as an essential part of running a safe organisation. The aim of the review should be to consider the operation of policies and procedures and any changes that should be made to prevent similar incidents occurring in the future. Reviews should take place on a regular (annual or twice-yearly) basis, after significant incidents have occurred, or where there have been changes to the working environment or function. This might result in:

* changes to the workplace;

* changes to working practices;

* new working procedures;

* additional training requirements.

KEY LEARNING POINTS

Incidents of violence and aggression have an impact on all those involved, including the worker, colleagues, managers and the perpetrator. This impact may be lasting if not managed effectively.

Team members and managers have a crucial role in supporting their colleagues after an incident. Managers have a role in reporting the incident, notifying partner agencies and deciding what action should be taken in respect of the perpetrator.

Employers in social care and health have a duty of care to their employees as set out in the GSCC Code of Practice (2010), and summarised in the UNISON guidance (nd).

TAKING IT FURTHER

General Social Care Council (GSCC) (2010) *Codes of Practice for Employers of Social Care Workers.* [online] Available at: www.scie.org.uk/workforce/careskillsbase/files/codesofpracticeforemployersofsocialcareworkers.pdf (accessed 26 April 2023).

NHS England (nd) Violence Prevention and Safety. [online] Available at: www.england.nhs.uk/supporting-our-nhs-people/health-and-wellbeing-programmes (accessed 26 April 2023).

UNISON (nd) *The UNISON Duty of Care Handbook.* [online] Available at: www.unison.org.uk/content/uploads/2013/06/On-line-Catalogue197863.pdf (accessed 6 April 2023).

Working with highly resistant families

INTRODUCTION

Over the past few years there has been concern about 'resistant' families in child protection caseloads who do not change and improve their parenting practice despite professional intervention. This is a significant issue as demonstrated in the 2005 to 2007 analysis of Serious Case Reviews which showed that 75 per cent of families involved were characterised as unco-operative, including hostility, avoidance, disguised compliance or ambivalence (Brandon et al, 2009).

Violence and aggression against protective workers is a key element of this resistance to intervention. The biennial analysis of Serious Case Reviews examined 161 cases. A sub-sample of 47 cases identified a continuum of co-operation between families and agencies. In 68 per cent of these case reviews there was evidence of a lack of co-operation from families, often manifested in overt hostility towards staff, including threats (Brandon et al, 2009). A more recent report by Brandon et al (2020) provides a more contemporary analysis of the challenges facing both families and practitioners in a world of reducing resources.

Much has recently been written about working with resistant families, which is beyond the scope of this book. It is nonetheless important to have an understanding of the mechanisms used by these families to resist professional interventions, some of which involve the use of intimidation and threat of violence.

In the child protection context it should also be remembered that some families have an understandable justification for resisting the interventions of social workers and other professionals, linked to their own negative experiences and the damage that can be caused by poor practice. These factors are taken into account systematically in approaches such as trauma-informed practice, and can help in working positively with such families.

TYPES OF RESISTANCE

Di Hart (2010) was commissioned by C4EO to undertake a thorough literature review on this topic. She identified four types of resistance in such families:

- ambivalence;

- denial/avoidance;

- unresponsiveness to treatment – families appear engaged but do not respond (disguised compliance);

- violence/hostility – intimidating to workers.

She also identified some key characteristics of families who are resistant to change, demonstrated by re-referral rates of 25 to 69 per cent in child protection systems. These characteristics include:

- families with a substantiated and repeated history of abuse – one of the most reliable predictors of resistance to intervention;

- multiple, simultaneous problems including domestic violence, substance misuse, mental health problems, criminal activity, lack of financial resources and poor support networks;

- lack of timely assessments and services.

The literature review identified evidence showing that practitioners involved in complex cases can lose focus on children when:

- the parents' needs override those of the children;

- parents are able to turn the focus away from maltreatment allegations;

- parents make it difficult for practitioners to see children alone.

These factors make it more difficult to conduct quality assessments due to insufficient information gathering and analysis, leading to poor decision-making and planning.

Intimidation, manipulation and the threat of violence are strategies used by some families to divert the focus of protective workers away from the children who are the subject of concern.

WORKING WITH RESISTANT FAMILIES

Brian Littlechild (2012) has highlighted the difficulty of working with resistant families. *'Working with resistant parents in child protection is one of the most difficult and risky enterprises in social work – for children, workers and agencies – as evidenced by research and child abuse death enquiry reports.'*

Littlechild (2008) also emphasises the impact of the intimidating context of protective work: *'There is a lot of fear which constrains what we do in child protection work. This is one of the most neglected areas of practice, and is not about targets and performance indicators. In 80 visits to Jasmine Beckford, workers never saw Jasmine alone'*.

In his article for *Community Care*, Littlechild (2020) further explores the theme of fear in social work and its impact on practice.

Other authors emphasise this point: '*There is an increased emphasis on investigative risk assessment focused work within what can often become situations of conflict*' (Parton, 1998): '*The set of procedures and guidelines has led to the social worker becoming an investigator, reporter and gatherer of evidence*' (Howe, 1992).

These procedures and guidelines do not always help the worker in the reality of their task.

There is an assumption in Working Together (HM Government, 2010) that parents and families are willing to be co-operative with protective workers. There is no mention of resistance, and its effects on assessment, plans and child focus, apart from one paragraph, 9.7: '*Some children may be living in families that are considered resistant to change.*'

Threats of violence to staff were judged to have contributed to Ainlee Walker's parents' elaborate concealment of abuse from the protection workers and partner agencies. These threats were also a major factor in the more recent cases involving Arthur Labinjo-Hughes and Star Hobson.

An assertive approach

The use of a confident, sensitive and assertive approach by the worker can be effective in breaking down resistance.

Ruth Pearson (2010) emphasises the importance of an assertive approach with a sensitive use of power. An assertive worker makes their opinions heard in a way that doesn't harm others, listens to the other's point of view without putting them down, has confident and appropriate body language and chooses the behaviour most appropriate to the situation.

Koprowska (2020) emphasises the skills and approach of the worker in successfully engaging with these families.

> *A key factor in securing engagement is the attitude and behaviour of the practitioner; most effective practitioners use their statutory powers in an honest and non-coercive manner while retaining scepticism and ability to challenge. An assertive, confident approach is needed.*

Good supervision and maintaining focus

Maintaining focus on the needs of children within their families has been seen as a key shortfall in practice common to many Serious Case Review reports, and has been identified by the Department for Education (DfE, 2022) as a practice theme requiring attention.

Good supervision is essential for all staff, and can help maintain focus on the needs of the child rather than the parents. Good supervision should also support reflective practice which can help untangle conflicting issues and maintain focus.

Hart's review (2010) also emphasised the need for effective supervision of safeguarding practice. She felt that good supervision is essential in all cases and in particular where practitioners:

- are overwhelmed or lacking confidence;

- have experienced violence;

- are acting out their own strong emotions.

The supervisor needs good knowledge and understanding of techniques for avoidance, and the importance of monitoring risk factors in management and supervision. Supervisors should be aware of fear of asserting control and surveillance as part of the dual role in child protection (support and surveillance). Checklists on these areas should be employed in supervision over time, during and after initial risk assessment and within risk management processes.

Good supervision can help address the acute problems of the rule of optimism; staff often wish to think the best of service users and to believe in their ability to change without the interventions of the professional. Parents who wish to can easily manipulate the worker through this mechanism.

Supervision is also essential to reduce the isolation of the worker. Isolation is a key factor in creating hostage syndrome and can lead to the worker being manipulated. Openness with the supervisor is also essential, and is dependent on the team culture. Not sharing information or concerns with the supervisor results in the supervisor not being aware of risks and the need to support the worker.

Lack of robust supervision was identified by Professor Eileen Munro as an issue in the Baby Peter case: '*robust supervision should have challenged this flawed appraisal*' (*Independent*, 2008). It should also help guard against the social worker's bias impairing judgement. This is a key role for knowledgeable, reflective practice in the supervision of child protection cases.

Littlechild (2010) states at paragraph 4.52:

> *supervision should enable both supervisor and supervisee to reflect on, scrutinise and evaluate the work carried out, assess the strengths and weaknesses of the practitioner in providing coaching, development and pastoral support. The supervisor should be available to practitioners as an important source of advice and expertise and may be required to endorse judgements at certain key points in the process.*

A key question in the supervision of child protection cases is: are there clear risk assessment procedures in place which take into account knowledge of avoidance, and the systematic planning and reviewing of the assessment and interventions over time, not just at initial referral?

STRENGTHS-BASED APPROACHES

Strengths-based approaches such as trauma-informed practice, strengthening families and signs of safety have become widely used in recent years. Trauma-informed practice recognises the prevalence of trauma and its impact on the emotional, psychological and social well-being of people. Having a basic understanding of how stress can affect an individual will make practitioners less likely to fuel other people's stress levels. Practitioners working in this way will pay attention to how they engage with people, thinking about what may have happened to them before rather than judging what is wrong with them.

Strengths-based approaches are used to help understand the impact of experiences in the past, and to make them explicit in considering future plans in conjunction with professionals. These approaches can demonstrate that the practitioner understands the experience of the family, which can go a long way to reduce stress and help develop a positive working relationship. This in turn will help defuse potential violence and aggression.

Although trauma-informed care is a relatively new concept in the child welfare system in the UK, similar principles underpin strengths and relationship-based practice models that have been implemented around the country. Examples include the following.

- **Restorative practices**, which focus on building respectful, collaborative relationships of challenge and support with a view to resolving difficulties and repairing harm.

- **Strengthening families and signs of safety**, which are strengths-based, solution-focused frameworks for collaborative engagement with families.

- **Family group conferences**, which is a family-led restorative practice that draws on the family network to safeguard children and support parents.

- **Motivational interviewing**, which helps parents to find the internal motivation they need to change their behaviour.

There is no doubt that to operate these approaches effectively takes a lot of time and resources, but can be ultimately be cost effective, particularly when access to formal protective services is appropriately managed.

It is important that within such approaches, which take into account the experiences of parents and carers, the priority remains the protection of vulnerable children and adults and is the reason for the intervention in the first place.

The effectiveness of this approach is exemplified by one local authority In my research for this edition. The authority has implemented a trauma-informed practice model which is supported by the local CAMHS Service. Child Protection and Children in Need services are co-located, and practitioners are required to physically attend the work base on at least three days per week. This helps to facilitate interaction between staff to help address the isolation caused by lockdowns and home-working during the pandemic.

Both individual and group supervision use a systemic therapeutic approach, and Support and Challenge panels are held regularly for practitioners to bring cases and dilemmas for discussion led by systemic family therapists in a group environment. This has been very successful in providing a safe and supportive space for workers. These discussions include trauma informed approaches to understanding family issues and behaviour, planning interventions and also address the psychological and physiological impact on workers of working in stressful situations.

This approach has been successful in supporting practitioners, and also in reducing the incidence of violence and aggression which is at a relatively low level in this authority. It has required a significant investment of interagency resources which has been justified by high levels of staff care, retention, agency performance and Ofsted gradings.

 KEY LEARNING POINTS

The issue of highly resistant families is associated with many Serious Case Review (Child Safeguarding Practice Reviews (CSPRs)) reports and a number of child deaths, including those of Ainlee Walker, Victoria Climbié, Peter Connelly, Star Hobson and Arthur Labinjo-Hughes.

Violence, intimidation and aggression is but one of the mechanisms used by resistant families.

Working with resistant families is one of the most difficult and challenging areas of social and healthcare work.

An assertive, confident and sensitive approach is required by workers involved with resistant families.

Workers need good, effective, knowledgeable supervision which gives scope for reflective practice, in order to deal with these complex issues and maintain focus on the child.

Strengths-based approaches such as trauma-informed practice, strengthening families and signs of safety can be used as a framework for these positive positive ways of working to reduce aggression and violence. Some authorities have introduced this very effectively.

Management of violence and aggression is not just about staff care and safety; it is also about the protection of children.

TAKING IT FURTHER

Brandon, M et al (2009) *Understanding Serious Case Reviews and Their Impact: A Biannual Analysis of Serious Case Reviews 2005–2007*. London: Department for Education.

Brandon, M et al (2020) Complexity and Challenge: A Triennial Analysis of SCRs 2014–2017. Department for Education. [online] Available at: https://assets.publishing.service.gov.uk/government/uploads/system/uploads/attachment_data/file/869586/TRIENNIAL_SCR_REPORT_2014_to_2017.pdf (accessed 22 June 2023).

Hart, D (2010) *Effective Practice to Protect Children Living in Highly Resistant Families: Implementing Lessons Learned from CC4EO's Knowledge Review*. Presentation to Community Care Conference, November.

HM Government (2018) Working Together to Safeguard Children: A Guide to Inter-agency Working to Safeguard and Promote the Welfare of Children. Updated version, July 2018. [online] Available at: https://assets.publishing.service.gov.uk/government/uploads/system/uploads/attachment_data/file/942454/Working_together_to_safeguard_children_inter_agency_guidance.pdf (accessed 25 June 2023).

Howe, D (1992) Child Abuse and the Bureaucratization of Social Work. *Sociological Review*, 40(3): 491–508.

Koprowska, J (2020) *Communication and Interpersonal Skills in Social Work*. Exeter: Learning Matters.

Parton, N (1998) Risk, Advanced Liberalism and Child Welfare: The Need to Rediscover Uncertainty and Ambiguity. *British Journal of Social Work*, 28(1): 5–27.

Pearson, R (2009) Working with Hostile or Uncooperative Families. In Hughes, E and Owen, H (eds) *Good Practice in Safeguarding Children*. London: Jessica Kingsley.

8 Working in non-responsive institutions

INTRODUCTION

This chapter will explore what practitioners can do when the issue of staff safety is not taken seriously by their managers. This will include approaches to proactively engage managers and politicians, as well as presentation of evidence, legal and duty of care aspects.

WORKPLACE CULTURE

The culture of an organisation or workplace defines and influences how it operates. It expresses itself in what it expects from staff, and in the care of staff in performing their duty. Many organisations have positive workplace cultures, look after their staff well, and perform well as organisations in meeting their aims. Organisations who do not look after their staff well tend not to perform well; this is almost inevitable as staff are the only means by which social care and health organisations can get their jobs done.

Unfortunately a positive workplace culture is not well developed in all social care organisations. In many such organisations, putting up with violence and aggression from service users is still seen as part of the job. Individual members of staff can be affected by this, and if they show concern about the level of violence and aggression they are seen as weak and not up to the job. As demonstrated earlier in this book, this is an unhealthy attitude, and one that will put staff at risk, increase levels of stress and reduce effective performance.

A positive workplace culture

Ray Braithwaite, writing in 2001, described a positive workplace culture which can reduce the level of aggression.

A positive workplace culture:

- offers a clear commitment to staff that violence at work is unacceptable;

- has a policy and procedure on violence at work which is known by all staff;

- has a simple user-friendly incident reporting form;

- takes a proactive stance to ensure that incidents do not occur;

- applies appropriate sanctions to perpetrators of violence;

- has a usable definition of violence and aggression;

- actively monitors all acts of aggression so as to identify trends, dangerous environments or dangerous people;

- takes appropriate action to stop recurrence;

- treats all acts of aggression towards staff seriously;

- does not minimise aggressive acts;

- provides legal advice for staff subjected to violence, informing them of their rights;

- provides personal insurance for staff, and compensation for those subjected to violence;

- ensures that comprehensive support is available via counselling and appropriate debriefing;

- provides training for staff on methods of managing aggression;

- proactively promotes a positive public image;

- believes that staff are the most important commodity the agency has and manages them as such.

If your organisation does not meet these standards, you are likely to be at risk. Fortunately there are a number of resources available to you which can be used to support the case for change. These are referred to below, and in Chapter 4.

UNISON

The trade union UNISON has produced a *Duty of Care Handbook* (nd) which sets out what employees can expect from their employing organisation, and also their own duty of care to their service users. This document is supported by the Health and Care Professions Council (HCPC) which regulates professionals in social care and health occupations, including social workers and health visitors.

Under current legislation, health and social care workplaces (which include visits to service users in their own homes or in the community) will have risk registers in place to record risks and provide a formal note of the action taken to manage these risks. These should contain information on existing procedures or controls that are in place to mitigate risks and what action should be taken if a risk arises.

Individual members of staff need to have the necessary experience or training to carry out their tasks safely; managers and supervisors should take responsibility for checking that tasks are only delegated to competent, well-equipped individuals.

It is important that planning for social care services should take into account the potential danger to staff and service users, and utilise risk assessment as part of the development programme. This, combined with high standards of service delivery and staff training, should ensure that the direct use of protective skills or restraint techniques is rarely required.

GOVERNMENT DOCUMENTS AND CODES OF PRACTICE

The Code of Practice for employers of social care workers, developed by the GSCC (2010), is at the time of writing held by SCIE. This document sets out the responsibilities of employers in the regulation of social care workers. Of specific relevance to staff safety, the code requires employers to have written policies and procedures in place to enable social care workers to meet their Code of Practice standards, including their responsibility for risk assessment, and enable social care workers to work in a safe environment. Employers also have a responsibility to effectively manage and supervise staff to support good practice.

Skills for Care has produced a leaflet entitled *Work Smart, Work Safe: Combating Violence against Care Staff: A Guide for Staff and Volunteers*, which build on and update the earlier Task Force documents. There are two sections:

1. a guide for staff and volunteers – this sets out the employer's primary responsibilities, questions which should be asked of employers and strategies to reduce risk;
2. a guide for employers – this sets out the key responsibilities of social care employers, and the measures they should take to reduce risks to their workers.

In addition to their duty of care to their employees, social care organisations have to take into account their care of service users, and the expectations of government bodies and professional organisations.

WHAT YOU CAN DO AS A PRACTITIONER IN HEALTH OR SOCIAL CARE

If the culture of your employing organisation does not support safe practice, there are a number of steps you can take.

1. Talk to your colleagues to see if this is an issue that also concerns them. If this is the case, put your concerns down on paper and take them to your manager for discussion in a team meeting or individually.

2. If your colleagues do not share your concerns, you should discuss them directly with your manager.
3. If the above steps do not produce any action, write to your trade union summarising your concerns, refer to the *Duty of Care Handbook* (UNISON, nd) and ask for a meeting.
4. If this matter cannot be resolved through the management chain, consider a direct approach to your organisation's governing body, which could be the appropriate committee of the council, the trustees of a charity or the management board of a private company.
5. If these approaches do not prove effective you could consider discussing with a specialist employment lawyer with a view to taking legal action. Such advice may be available at no charge for a first appointment.

 KEY LEARNING POINTS

If your workplace (which includes visits in the community) does not have a positive culture promoting staff safety and safe practice, you should seek to take action to protect yourself as a professional and also to provide better-quality services to the vulnerable people you look after.

If your employer expects you to work in an unsafe environment, and does not take steps to minimise risk, you should discuss the situation with your colleagues. The documents listed below provide a basis for taking action.

The UNISON (nd) *Duty of Care Handbook* gives clear guidance as to what you can expect from your employers, and what their responsibilities are for supporting and protecting staff.

Skills for Care leaflets are available, summarising the rights of employees and the duties of employers.

Safe working not only protects workers, but also helps protect vulnerable clients.

TAKING IT FURTHER

SCIE. *Work Smart, Work Safe: Combating Violence against Care Staff: A Guide for Staff and Volunteers*. [online] Available at: www.learningsupportcentre.com/wp-content/uploads/2014/09/Skills-for-care-Work-smart-work-safe-guide-for-employees.pdf (accessed 22 June 2023).

UNISON (nd) *The UNISON Duty of Care Handbook*. [online] Available at: www.unison.org.uk/content/ uploads/2013/06/Online-Catalogue197863.pdf (accessed 6 April 2023).

9 Performance management in social care

INTRODUCTION

Performance management in social care and health services is about getting the best services and outcomes from available resources, whether as a single agency or working with partners to achieve this. It is a key priority for senior and middle managers in social care and health organisations, and can help significantly improve practice in the protection of vulnerable people.

There are two basic types of performance management:

- organisational performance measured against standards, targets and comparator organisations;

- individual performance of staff and managers, preferably measured against competency frameworks.

In social care and health services, staff are the primary means through which services are delivered and quality is provided. The organisation cannot function without them, or provide quality services without their active contributions. Staff perform better when supported, well supervised, trained, provided with appropriate resources and enabled to practise safely. They are also professionals, personally responsible for meeting professional standards, and should be held accountable for their practice.

A performance management framework should ensure that staff are properly supported and held accountable, and that their activities are directed toward meeting the required outcomes of the service overall. A fully functioning performance framework should be able to quickly identify shortfalls in individual and corporate practice, and enable a timely correctional response from leaders and managers.

The earlier chapters of this book provide evidence that individual staff performance, particularly in child protection situations, is significantly affected by working in stressful and unsafe family contexts. This will in turn affect the performance of the service overall, and it is therefore argued that promotion of staff safety is a significant factor in delivering improved performance. Training in staff safety and safe working practice should be routinely part of the overall package of support for professionals, alongside training in assessment and care planning, as a key skills set.

PERFORMANCE MANAGEMENT IN RELATION TO STAFF SAFETY

To promote staff safety through performance management frameworks, two key elements need to be in place:

1.   competence and accountability frameworks for individual professional staff;
2.   a performance framework which can be used to monitor, evaluate and improve the performance of the service overall in achieving its required outcomes.

Competence and accountability frameworks for individual professionals

All training, support and accountability processes for individual professionals should be based on an agreed competency framework, tailored to individual roles within the service. Such a competency framework should clearly include staff safety skills and knowledge for practitioners, supervisors and managers. This framework could then underpin the following activities.

Development of Newly Qualified Social Workers (NQSWs)

NQSWs working within the Assessed and Supported Year in Employment (ASYE) programme are guided by the Professional Capabilities Framework (PCF) which is a useful competency framework. This does not specifically address personal safety issues, but does recognise the stress placed on workers by adverse environments. Personal safety could be usefully incorporated into this framework.

Staff training for social workers and health professionals

Training needs assessments should be carried out against a competency framework and shortfalls identified. Training in staff safety should be a key element in this.

Supervision training

Supervision training should include awareness of the impact of working with potentially violent and aggressive service users on professional practice and decision-making. It should include skills, techniques and systems for ensuring the safety of practitioners, including risk assessments of individual service users, and of activities within the job. It should also include training in reflective practice, which can help manage the impact of violence and aggression.

Management training

Management training should include responsibilities and accountability of managers for promoting staff safety, and ways in which this can be promoted.

Resources and work environment

The work environment should support staff safety. Offices should be provided with interview rooms containing alarm systems, notices publicising the policy of zero tolerance of abuse to staff, and trained reception staff who are able to recognise and defuse potential aggression. There should be a lone working policy, which includes safety arrangements for staff visiting in the community, and team-based support systems. Professionals should be provided with mobile phones and security alarms for use in an emergency.

Recording of incidents

A process should be in place for recording all incidents of violence and aggression, both verbal and physical, whether taking place on office premises, in the community or in service users' homes. Reports from this system should be considered by senior management at regular intervals, and any necessary remedial action taken.

Positive publicity

Social care and health organisations should promote a positive image of their service through developing local publicity, websites and positive communication with the press and media. Such a positive image should help reduce the propensity for abuse of social care and health professionals involved in child protection.

ORGANISATIONAL PERFORMANCE

Organisational performance management focuses on providing quality services which meet standards, achieve set aims and deliver the required outcomes of service overall. It will be monitored and evaluated by internal audit and external inspection regimes, including Ofsted and the Care Quality Commission (CQC). Organisational performance will be dependent on the cumulative activity of practitioners, supervisors and managers, and on the effectiveness of the systems in which they operate.

Statutory performance measures tend to be proxy indicators of service quality. Arguably, if a service is of a high quality, this should be reflected in its performance measures. Unfortunately this is not always the case, and it is essential to make good practice visible through these indicators to help achieve a positive evaluation from inspectors.

The performance measures in the following areas are relevant to staff safety in child protection work.

Assessment and care planning

At the time of writing, a number of performance measures are used to monitor performance in assessment. These include timescales for completion of assessments, and are also judged on:

- performance in gathering information: assessed by the quality and completeness of recording and the depth of information acquired. This is dependent on the practitioner being able to access robust information from the service user, and will be affected by actions to resist involvement, including the use of violence and aggression. Practitioners who feel confident in challenging situations will be more effective in gathering the required detailed information;

- the quality of recording of information for assessment on the case record;

- analysis of information collected: dependent on the quality of information available for analysis, as well as the quality of the analysis itself and how it is recorded;

- planning: evidence that the plan is based on the assessment and clearly recorded. The analysis and plan should be shared with the service user, which will require a confident relationship in challenging circumstances.

Effective practice in assessment and care planning will to some extent be dependent on robust staff support and safety systems, which can help improve quality when working with challenging families.

Reports to child and adult protection conferences

Good practice in providing reports to initial and review child protection conferences will require a high standard of information gathering, analysis and planning. It also requires practitioners to be able to discuss their analysis and recommendations with the service user's family prior to the conference. This will benefit from a confident, assertive approach from the practitioner, informed by risk assessments and any necessary steps to ensure safe practice. Staff safety systems and training will support this.

Management of child and adult protection conferences

Child protection conferences are forums where important and lasting decisions are made about children and their families. They can be meetings where strong feelings are expressed, sometimes in an aggressive or intimidating way. It is important that child protection chairs and conference organisers are familiar with safe practice approaches, can risk-assess such conferences in advance, and take necessary precautions to ensure that meetings are not disrupted. This may involve meeting different parts of the family separately. Chairs will also need to be confident in using assertive practice in their chairing role. These practices will help to improve the quality of conference organisation and conduct, and will be subject to observation by inspectors. Consistent safe practice will provide positive evidence for such an inspection.

Monitoring and surveillance in child and adult protection

Monitoring and surveillance are essential elements of a child protection plan. They will require the completion of a number of specified tasks including:

- child and adult protection visits to families, both announced and unannounced;

- seeing children and vulnerable adults alone;

- inspecting bedrooms and other parts of the accommodation.

Successful completion of these tasks will require a confident, assertive and respectful approach, which takes into account the impact of any intimidation or aggression used by the family to prevent effective surveillance. As noted previously, these have been significant factors in some child deaths, where effective surveillance has been thwarted by these means.

CORE GROUPS

Core groups are where professionals, family members and significant others meet to discuss progress on the child protection plan. They can be places where aggression or intimidation is shown by family members, which will need to be managed effectively to achieve a productive outcome. Safe practice procedures and training will help manage this process, and help evidence good core group practice overall.

COURTS AND CARE PROCEEDINGS

Family courts are where care proceedings are heard, and are dependent on reports, evidence and testimony from social care and health practitioners. This can cause significant anxiety, not only from the stress involved in giving evidence, but also from anxiety about the physical safety of workers, and exposure to intimidation and aggression. Courts are able to make special arrangements in circumstances where there is likely to be disruption, and practitioners need to be aware of this, and who to contact in the court to make such arrangements. These may include security screens, separate entrances, and video testimony from vulnerable children and young people. Safe practice approaches and training should incorporate knowledge of this provision.

KEY LEARNING POINTS

Performance of social care and health organisations depends largely on the cumulative individual performance of their staff.

The performance of individual staff in child protection and other stress-inducing work is in turn dependent on feeling safe and protected in the work environment.

Staff safety and safe practice should be built into professional competence frameworks, and supported by training and development programmes.

Performance at each stage of child protection and similar processes can be enhanced by staff safety and safe practice training.

10 Working effectively in stressful situations: putting it all together

The focus of this book is not just to help social care and health workers to stay safe in challenging situations, but also to help them work effectively to protect vulnerable people, both adults and children. This chapter brings together the issues and learning from the previous chapters into a practical guide to working effectively. The principles not only relate to working in stressful situations, but are basically a development of good practice which can be used in every case.

To work safely and effectively it is necessary for the employing organisation to ensure that caseloads and intake rates are kept at a level within the capacity of teams and individual workers. The definition of this may vary from organisation to organisation, and will be dependent on the resources available, but it is an essential precondition of effective working. It is the responsibility of the agency to provide this situation through the effective use of systems and processes, both single and multi-agency.

A FRAMEWORK FOR SAFE AND EFFECTIVE WORKING

Working safely and effectively is an organisational and team issue and not just the responsibility of the practitioner. All agencies and partners in protective services have a duty to ensure the safety of their staff and their ability to work effectively in protecting vulnerable people. These duties can be considered under the following role headings:

- practitioner;

- supervisor;

- team;

- agency/organisation;

- inspector;

- local government;

- national government.

Practitioner

Training and professional development

- Ensure that you have taken up opportunities for training in strengths-based approaches to working with families, to help understand their formative experiences and the potential impact on their behaviour.

- Take up any opportunities available for personal safety training in the context of your work.

Preparation in advance of visits to and contact with service users

- Evaluate any information known about service users from file records, interagency intelligence or social media, and identify any risks to your safety. This is important for both initial visits and ongoing contact.

- Be aware of safety issues involved in visiting the client, including transport arrangements and the location/layout of the client's home, or interview facility.

- Conduct a risk assessment using this information and share with your supervisor or colleague.

- Use any additional resource necessary to maintain your safety including joint visiting with a colleague, another agency staff member, or police.

- Be familiar with the use of safety equipment, including mobile phone applications, team-based code words, attack alarms and backup resources available to you.

- Ask yourself 'What do I need to get from this visit/interview?' 'What does the service user need?' Be clear what information you need and what the service user needs. Who do you need to talk to or see (including the child or vulnerable person)?

- Decide how you are going to communicate this to the service user, including practising words and phrases.

- Decide how you are going to end the visit and leave the service user's home/interview facility.

Onsite

- Make sure you arrive on time and have any necessary information with you.

- Maintain your safety awareness and conduct a dynamic risk assessment throughout contact.

- Make sure you understand the client's perspective and treat them in a respectful way.

- Maintain your focus on the task, the issues you need to discuss and the information you need to obtain.

- Keep calm and make sure you give the client any necessary information in a clear and unambiguous way.

- Take any necessary notes in an open but unobtrusive way. Explain clearly your reasons for doing this.

After the visit (at the office or at home)

- Complete case recording.

- Report any incidents involving health and safety, and the personal impact on yourself.

- Seek support from a supervisor or colleague if needed.

- Debrief as necessary with your supervisor.

Supervisor

As supervisor you are the primary support of your worker.

- In supervision you should help your worker prepare for potentially stressful visits using the format above.

- You should be open to any concerns or fears expressed by the worker and help work through them without any negativity. Take any necessary supportive and preventive actions.

- Review cases regularly to ensure that none are missed due to reluctance to report.

- Routinely check your worker's case notes to identify risk factors.

- Debrief your worker after any situation involving violence, threat or intimidation.

- You should try to be available for any necessary ad hoc consultation prior to a visit by your supervisee including assisting with a risk assessment.

Team

As team manager you should organise regular team discussions focusing on practice issues including working effectively in stressful situations.

- All team members, and not just the team manager, have a responsibility for the safety and well-being of their colleagues and should participate in team-based discussions on the subject as a priority.

- Team discussion should focus also on developing approaches which value the service user's experience such as trauma-informed practice, systemic supervision and strengths-based interventions. These can help reduce risk factors, obtain good information and lead to more effective practice.

- Teams should routinely share and discuss information about their clients on a confidential professional basis, including information about risks and dangers from the family and the community, and information from other agencies. Information from other agencies will be crucial to this.

- Teams should practise working in difficult situations and stressful environments including working on scenarios, scripts and checklists.

- The team should routinely discuss their use of social media on both a professional and personal basis, and develop agreed ways of using them within the team and outside the team.

Agency/organisation

The agency has a duty of care to its employees, which includes a duty to help them be able to work safely. This duty, backed up by law, requires agencies to provide a reasonable working environment for staff which in the social care context can include the following.

- Keeping caseloads to manageable levels through active management of intake and the recruitment of appropriate levels of staffing and supervision.

- Developing and training staff in the use of strengths-based approaches and trauma-informed practice.

- Providing training in safe and effective working in the professional context.

- Providing policies and procedures in risk assessment and lone working.

- Maintaining records of incidents of violence and aggression towards social care and healthcare staff, and taking any necessary action.

- Providing regular audits of the standards of staff care and safety throughout the organisation (see page 40).

Inspector

- Inspection agencies including Ofsted and CQC could consider, as part of their process, the impact on staff of fear induced by threat, intimidation and violence on their ability to work effectively to protect vulnerable children and adults.

- It might be helpful if inspection agencies were to introduce a thematic review of the impact of violence and aggression on protective practice, and recommend any steps which could be taken to improve the standard of work in such challenging areas.

Local and national government

At the time of writing, the UK government has introduced a wide-ranging review of children's services practice, currently subject to consultation. This is a welcome initiative which should include addressing the impact of violence and aggression on protective practice.

11   Summary of issues

FINAL THOUGHTS

Working as a frontline practitioner in social care or health services is a difficult, essential and potentially rewarding job. Working in child or adult protection or in mental health services further adds to the complexity of the task, and is often conducted in a stressful and risky environment.

Social workers and health professionals need to be mature, sensitive and confident individuals, able to give clear messages to their clients and challenge poor or dangerous parenting and care. It is one of the most challenging jobs in the country, and requires great personal strength to conduct it effectively.

Workers not only need to utilise their professional training and skills in information gathering, assessment, analysis and planning interventions, but also to be able to explain to service users exactly what they are doing, and to present well-reasoned and evidenced cases in court. The role of the protective worker is therefore demanding enough, without the added stress of threats, intimidation and violence from the families of the children and vulnerable adults they help to protect.

It is the main theme of this book that these practitioners need to be trained, supported and protected by their employers and colleagues, not only from the perspective of good staff care, but also to equip them to effectively undertake their job and to improve the performance of their service in caring for vulnerable people.

SUMMARY OF CHAPTERS

Chapter 1: The extent of violence against social care workers and health professionals

This chapter summarises the extent of violence and aggression against social care and health staff which has continued to increase since the 1970s, despite a number of campaigns and government initiatives to address the issue.

The issue is not about isolated attacks on professionals, serious as these are, but is more about endemic and widespread threats of violence to very large numbers of staff in health and social care. These are part of the working life of workers in adult and child protection and mental health services.

Chapter 2: The physiological and psychological impact of violence and intimidation on professional decision-making

This chapter examines the physiological and psychological impact of stress and the threat of violence on the body. An automatic, hormone-induced response leads to a freeze, flight or fight reaction to safeguard the body from physical harm. The downside of this is a devastating effect on the ability to think clearly, analyse situations and make professional judgements.

Long-term intimidation of isolated protective workers can create a hostage-like situation, where the professional identifies with the family, minimises evidence of risk to the child, and ceases to be able to use objective judgement in the protection task.

The role of men in families is often minimised by practitioners. Fathers can remain physically absent yet highly influential and can present a potent threat of violence. Fear of this may be one of the factors that result in practitioners avoiding working directly with fathers and other significant males.

The chapter emphasises the fact that working in a potentially dangerous environment not only puts the individual professional at risk, but also severely impacts on their ability to do their job effectively, and to protect the children they work with.

Chapter 3: What practitioners can do to keep themselves safe

Chapter 3 looks at how practitioners can look after themselves and keep safe when doing their work in the office, in their own homes, in the communities and travelling to visits. It highlights the importance of risk assessments both of the people involved in the case and of the scenarios they are likely to be involved in, which may include having to see children alone or giving unwelcome news. Understanding the causes and motivations behind aggressive behaviour is essential in keeping safe and being able to perform the protective task effectively. The role of team members in looking after each other is emphasised, including team safety systems and building on the training they may have received.

Chapter 4: What organisations can do to keep staff safe

Social care and health organisations have a statutory duty of care to their employees, and are required by the Skills for Care codes of practice to put in place a range of systems and supports to help keep them safe in the course of their work. Similar arrangements are in place for health employees, under NHS regulations. This chapter argues that it is necessary for employers to go beyond the minimum, and actively promote staff safety from the top to the bottom of the organisation. The provision of training and supervision in strengths-based approaches will support staff to keep safe and work well. This will ultimately benefit the overall performance of the service, which is dependent on the well-being and motivation of staff.

Chapter 5: Keeping safe in an incident

This chapter explores what practitioners can do personally if they find themselves in a situation of violence or aggression. It looks at where this behaviour might be coming from and what it seeks to achieve, and ways of defusing and de-escalating the situation. Through an exploration of body language it can help practitioners understand where it is safe to remain in a situation and negotiate, and recognise where it is too dangerous and they should leave for their own physical safety. The role of practitioners in unnecessarily escalating situations is explored, together with ways in which they can model positive behaviour to resolve the situation. The use of physical disengagement techniques is discussed, the most important of which is maintaining safe distance from a potential aggressor at a time of crisis. The chapter concludes with an examination of the psychological and emotional impact of a violent incident on both the worker and the service user.

Chapter 6: Post-incident responses

The emotional impact of a violent incident was covered in the previous chapter. This chapter examines what team members and managers should do to support their colleagues following such an event. This ranges from emotional support to meeting procedural requirements for reporting. Effective post-incident support can greatly help practitioners to recover and move on from such a distressing incident.

Chapter 7: Working with highly resistant families

The use of violence, threats and intimidation is but one means by which families resist change and the interventions of professionals. This chapter argues that it is necessary to understand other strategies employed by families, and how they link with the threat of violence and aggression. It also looks at the use of trauma-informed practice, strengths-based approaches and an assertive approach by the practitioner as the most effective in securing change in resistant families.

Chapter 8: Working in non-responsive institutions

Employers of social care and health practitioners have a duty of care to their staff, which is not always prioritised by their organisations. This chapter gives practitioners working in such organisations advice on how they can stimulate awareness and change with their managers and governing bodies. This is not only to protect staff, but also to provide a better service to vulnerable children and adults, and to improve the reputation of the organisation overall.

Chapter 9: Performance management in social care

The performance of social care and health organisations is largely dependent on the cumulative performance of individual staff. This chapter explores the impact of effective staff safety arrangements on performance throughout the child and adult protection system, from assessment through case conference to the implementation of protection plans. This will help social care and partner organisations to meet statutory requirements and improve inspection ratings.

Chapter 10: Working effectively in stressful situations: putting it all together

This chapter brings together the key themes from the book into a framework for safe and effective working in challenging and potentially dangerous situations. Safe working is not just the responsibility of the individual worker and this chapter summarises the actions that practitioners, supervisors, teams, agencies and employers can take together to provide a safe working environment, which is also better for the people for whom services are being provided. It also suggests the roles that inspection agencies and government could take to promote and monitor safe and effective working in this critical sector.

Bibliography

American Federation of Government Employees (AFGE) (2016) Violence Against Health & Social Service Workers. [online] Available at: www.afge.org/article/violence-against-health-care--social-service-workers-must-end (accessed 26 April 2023).

BASW (2010) BASW backs Khyra Ishaq Review and Urges Investment in Social Work to Minimise Risk of Future Tragedies. [online] Available at: www.basw.co.uk/media/news/2010/jul/basw-backs-khyra-ishaq-review-and-urges-investment-social-work-minimise-risk (accessed 22 June 2023).

BASW Northern Ireland (2018) Insult and Injury: Exploring the Impacts of Intimidation, Threats and Violence against Social Workers. Belfast: BASW. [online] Available at: www.basw.co.uk/system/files/resources/insult-injury-social-workers.pdf (accessed 26 April 2023).

Biestek, F R (1957) *The Casework Relationship*. Chicago: Loyola University Press.

Biggart, L, Ward, E, Cook, L, Stride, C, Schofield, G, Corr, P, Fletcher, C, Bowler, J, Jordan, P and Bailey, S (2016) *Emotional Intelligence and Burnout in Child and Family Social Work: Implications for Policy and Practice*. Norwich: Centre for Research on Children and Families. [online] Available at: www.basw.co.uk/system/files/resources/basw_92559-3_0.pdf (accessed 20 April 2023).

Braithwaite, R (2001) *Managing Aggression*. London: Routledge (in association with *Community Care*).

Brandon, M et al (2009) *Understanding Serious Case Reviews and Their Impact: A Biannual Analysis of Serious Case Reviews 2005–2007*. London: Department for Education.

Brandon, M et al (2020) Complexity and Challenge: A Triennial Analysis of SCRS 2014–2017. Department for Education. [online] Available at: https://assets.publishing.service.gov.uk/government/uploads/system/uploads/attachment_data/file/869586/TRIENNIAL_SCR_REPORT_2014_to_2017.pdf (accessed 22 June 2023).

Department for Education (2019) PSDP–Resouces and Tools: Having Reflective Discussion in Supervision. [online] Available at: https://practice-supervisors.rip.org.uk/wp-content/uploads/2019/11/Having-reflective-discussions-in-supervision.pdf (accessed 25 June 2023).

Department of Health (2000) *A Safer Place: Combating Violence against Social Care Staff. Report of the Task Force and National Action Plan*. London: Department of Health.

Department of Health (2001) *A Safer Place: Self Audit Tool for Employers: Combating Violence against Social Care Staff*. London: Department of Health.

Department of Health (2001) *National Task Force on Violence against Social Care Staff*. London: Department of Health.

Farmer, E and Owen, M (1995) *Child Protection Practice: Private Risks and Public Remedies. Decision-making, Intervention and Outcome in Child Protection Work*. London: HMSO.

Figley, C R (ed) (1995) *Compassion Fatigue: Coping with Secondary Traumatic Stress Disorder in Those Who Treat the Traumatized*. New York: Brunner/Mazel.

Figley, C R (2012) Helping that Hurts: Child Welfare Secondary Traumatic Stress Reactions. In LaLiberte, T and Crudo, T (eds) *CW360. A Comprehensive Look at a Prevalent Child Welfare Issue: Secondary Trauma and the Child Welfare Workforce* (pp 4–5). Center for Advanced Studies in Child Welfare, School of Social Work, University of Minnesota. [online] Available at: https://ovc.ojp.gov/sites/g/files/xyckuh226/files/media/document/os_sts_child_welfare_article_review.pdf (accessed 20 April 2023).

General Social Care Council (GSCC) (2010) *Codes of Practice for Employers of Social Care Workers.* [online] Available at: www.scie.org.uk/workforce/careskillsbase/files/codesofpracticeforemployersofsocial-careworkers.pdf (accessed 6 April 2023).

Gov.uk (2022) National Review into the Murders of Arthur Labinjo-Hughes and Star Hobson. Child Safeguarding Practice Review Panel. [online] Available at: www.gov.uk/government/publications/national-review-into-the-murders-of-arthur-labinjo-hughes-and-star-hobson (accessed 26 April 2023).

Hart, D (2010) *Effective Practice to Protect Children Living in Highly Resistant Families: Implementing Lessons Learned from CC4EO's Knowledge Review.* Presentation to Community Care Conference, November.

Health and Safety Executive (HSE) (2009) *Improving Health and Safety Performance in the Health and Social Care Sectors – Next Steps?* HSE Board paper no. HSE/09/84, 23 September.

Health and Safety Executive (HSE) (2022) Violence at Work, 2019/20. [online] Available at: www.hse.gov.uk/statistics/causinj/violence/index.htm (accessed 22 June 2023).

Healy, K (1998) Participation and Child Protection: The Importance of Context. *British Journal of Social Work*, 28(6): 897–914.

Hendricks, A (2012) Secondary Traumatic Stress in Child Welfare: Multi-level Prevention and Intervention Strategies. In LaLiberte, T and Crudo, T (eds) *CW360. A Comprehensive Look at a Prevalent Child Welfare Issue: Secondary Trauma and the Child Welfare Workforce* (pp 12–13). Center for Advanced Studies in Child Welfare, School of Social Work, University of Minnesota. [online] Available at: https://ovc.ojp.gov/sites/g/files/xyckuh226/files/media/document/os_sts_child_welfare_article_review.pdf (accessed 20 April 2023).

Herman, J (1992) *Trauma and Recovery: The Aftermath of Violence – From Domestic Abuse to Political Terror.* New York: Basic Books.

Her Majesty's Stationery Office (HMSO) (1995) *Child Protection: Messages from Research.* London: HMSO.

HM Government (2010) Working Together to Safeguard Children: A Guide to Inter-agency Working to Safeguard and Promote the Welfare of Children. HM Government: London.

Howe, D (1992) Child Abuse and the Bureaucratization of Social Work. *Sociological Review*, 40(3): 491–508.

Independent (2008) Eileen Munro: Lessons Learnt, Boxes Ticked, Families Ignored. [online] Available at: www.independent.co.uk/voices/commentators/eileen-munro-lessons-learnt-boxes-ticked-families-ignored-1020508.html (accessed 22 June 2023).

Kaplan, S and Wheeler, E (1983) Survival Skills for Working with Potentially Violent Clients. Social Casework. *Journal of Contemporary Social Work*, 64(6): 339–46.

Kinoglu, S, Nelson-Dusek, S and Skrypek, M (2017) Creating a Trauma-informed Organization. Saint Paul, MN: Wilder Foundation. [online] Available at: www.wilder.org/sites/default/files/imports/VOA_TraumaReport_1–17.pdf (accessed 20 April 2023).

Koprowska, J (2020) *Communication and Interpersonal Skills in Social Work.* Exeter: Learning Matters.

Leadbetter, D and Trewartha, R (1996) *Handling Violence and Aggression at Work.* Lyme Regis: Russell House Publishing.

Littlechild, B (2008) Child Protection Social Work: Risks of Fears and Fears of Risks – Impossible Tasks from Impossible Goals? *Social Policy and Administration*, 42(6): 662–75.

Littlechild, B (2012) Working with Resistant Parents in Child Protection: Recognising and Responding to the Risks. *Joint World Conference on Social Work and Social Development.*

Littlechild, B (2020) Managing Fear in Social Work. *Community Care*, 18 November. [online] Available at: www.ccinform.co.uk/practice-guidance/managing-fear-in-social-work/ (accessed 26 April 2023).

Local Government Association (LGA) (2007) *Assaults on Social Care Staff at 'Unacceptable Levels' Warns LGA.* LGA press release, 20 October.

Lord Laming (2003) *Victoria Climbié Inquiry Report*. London: Department of Health.

McBride, P (1998) *The Assertive Social Worker*. Aldershot: Arena.

Mehrabian, A (1981) *Silent Messages: Implicit Communication of Emotions and Attitudes*. Belmont, CA: Wadsworth.

Mikulincer, M (1994) *Human Learned Helplessness: A Coping Perspective*. New York: Plenum Press.

Millham, S and Bullock, R (1976) *New Residential Approaches*. Proceedings of 1976 conference, Association for the Psychiatric Study of Adolescence.

Morris, E K, Smith, N G and Altus, D E (2005) B. F. Skinner's Contributions to Applied Behavior Analysis. *The Behavior Analyst*, 28(2): 99–131.

Navarro, J and Karlins, M (2008) *What Every Body Is Saying*. New York: Harper.

NHS (2021) NHS Staff Survey 2021. [online] Available at: www.nhsstaffsurveys.com/results/results-archive (accessed 26 April 2023).

NHS Security Management Service (2009) *Not Alone: A Guide for the Better Protection of Lone Workers in the NHS*. London: NHS. [online] Available at: www.nhsemployers.org/publications/improving-personal-safety-lone-workers (accessed 22 June 2023).

O'Hagan, K (1997) The Problem of Engaging Men in Child Protection Work. *British Journal of Social Work*, 27(1): 25–42.

Parton, N (1998) Risk, Advanced Liberalism and Child Welfare: The Need to Rediscover Uncertainty and Ambiguity. *British Journal of Social Work*, 28(1): 5–27.

Pearson, R (2009) Working with Unco-operative or Hostile Families. In Hughes, E and Owen, H (eds) *Good Practice in Safeguarding Children* (pp 85–102). London: Jessica Kingsley.

Pearson, R (2010) *Getting through the Door: Working with Overtly Uncooperative Clients to Move Past Barriers*. Presentation to Community Care Conference, November.

Perlman, H H (1979) *Relationship: The Heart of Helping People*. Chicago: University of Chicago Press.

Quinn, A, Ji, P and Nackerud, L (2018) Predictors of Secondary Traumatic Stress Among Social Workers: Supervision, Income and Caseload Size. *Journal of Social Work*, 19(4): 504–28.

Reder, P, Duncan, S and Gray, M (1993) *Beyond Blame: Child Abuse Tragedies Revisited*. London: Routledge.

Richmond, M (1917) *Social Diagnosis*. New York: Russell Sage Foundation.

Ross, R G (2007) *Personal Safety and Self Defence*. London: Teach Yourself.

Rowett, C (1986) *Violence in Social Work: A Research Study of Violence in the Context of Local Authority Social Work*. Cambridge: University of Cambridge Institute of Criminology.

Seddon, J (2003) *Freedom from Command and Control: A Better Way to Make Work Work*. Buckingham: Vanguard Consulting Ltd.

Skills for Care (nd) *Work Smart, Work Safe: Combating Violence against Care Staff: A Guide for Staff and Volunteers*. [online] Available at: www.learningsupportcentre.com/wp-content/uploads/2014/09/Skills-for-care-Work-smart-work-safe-guide-for-employees.pdf (accessed 22 June 2023).

Social Work News (2022) Social Workers Forced out of Homes due to abuse After Arthur Labinjo-Hughes Case. 26 May. [online] Available at: www.mysocialworknews.com/article/social-workers-forced-out-of-homes-due-to-abuse-after-arthur-labinjo-hughes-case (accessed 26 April 2023).

Stanley, J and Goddard, C (2007) *In the Firing Line: Violence and Power in Child Protection Work*. Chichester: Wiley.

Thompson, N, Murphy, M and Stradling, S (1994) *Dealing with Stress*. Basingstoke: Macmillan.

Tullberg, E, Avinadav, R and Chemtob, C M (2012) Going Beyond Self-care: Effectively Addressing Secondary Traumatic Stress Among Child Protective Staff. In LaLiberte, T and Crudo, T (eds) *CW360. A Comprehensive Look at a Prevalent Child Welfare Issue: Secondary Trauma and the Child Welfare Workforce* (p 22). Center for Advanced Studies in Child Welfare, School of Social Work, University of Minnesota. [online] Available at: https://ovc.ojp.gov/sites/g/files/xyckuh226/files/media/document/os_sts_child_welfare_article_review.pdf (accessed 20 April 2023).

UNISON (nd) *The UNISON Duty of Care Handbook*. [online] Available at: www.unison.org.uk/content/uploads/2013/06/On-line-Catalogue197863.pdf (accessed 6 April 2023).

UNISON (2008) *Time for a Change*. London: UNISON.

UNISON (2022) Manifesto for Social Workers 2021. London: UNISON. [online] Available at: www.unison.org.uk/content/uploads/2022/03/UNISON-Social-Work-Manifesto-2021.pdf (accessed 6 April 2023).

United States Bureau of Labor Statistics (2020) Injuries, Illnesses, and Fatalities Fact Sheet: Workplace Violence in Healthcare, 2018. [online] Available at: www.bls.gov/iif/factsheets/workplace-violence-health-care-2018.htm (accessed 26 April 2023).

Index

ABC method of behaviour analysis, 57, 58
Adverse Childhood Experiences (ACEs), 56
agencies/organisations, duty of care, 104–5
aggression. *See* violence and aggression
anxiety, through social media, 3
automatic response, 18

baseline behaviour, 59–60
Batari's Box, 64–5
body language, 63–7, 69, 85, 108
breakaway training, basic, 72

child death enquiries, 20
child protection, problem of practitioners
    in, 20
Code of Practice, 44, 48, 79, 92
competence and accountability frameworks,
    96–7
complaints, misuse of, 4
conflict management techniques, 67–9
  apologising, 68
  application of, 64
  giving information, 68
  giving space, 68
  humour, 69
  listening, 68
  removing audience, 68
  sitting down, 69
  staying calm, 69
  understanding, 68
coping strategies, 26–7
  avoidance, 26
  problem-solving, 26
  reappraisal, 26
  reorganisation, 26
  and task performance, 26

danger signs, 66–7
de-escalation techniques, 69–70

domestic violence, on children, 19–20
drugs and alcohol use, 19
duty of care to staff, 79–81
  colleagues, support from, 79
  debriefing, 80
  management responses, 80–1
  managers, support from, 79–80

emotional arousal, 59
  baseline behaviour, 59–60
  crisis phase, 61
  escalation phase, 61
  post-crisis depression stage, 61
  recovery phase, 61
  trigger phase, 60
emotional well-being, impact on, 5–6
employers
  key questions, 42
  key responsibilities, 48–52
  self-audit, 48–52
  service users, duty of care to, 43–4
  staff, duty of care to, 79–81
  support for staff, 45–6

facial expression, 64
family group conferences, 87
freeze, fight or flight response, 17–18, 62
Functional Behavioural Analysis, 57–8

Health and Care Professions Council
    (HCPC), 91
Hobson, Star, 6
hostage theory, 24–5, 107
  broader impact, 27–8
  coping strategies, 26–7
  implications, 28
  research findings, 28
  Stockholm Syndrome, 25
  and supervision, 45, 52

terrorist hostages compared with child
protection, 27

inspectors, 105
intimidating behaviour, 3–4, 10, 17

job context, 20–1
maintaining contact, 21
pressure, 20
procedures, 20–1

Labinjo-Hughes, Arthur, 6
lone working and staff safety policies, 48

managing an incident aims, 57–9
causes of violent behaviour, 55–7
key post-crisis reactions, 61
media, spotlight, 4
motivational interviewing, 87
multi-agency working practices, 28, 52

National Task Force on Violence against Social
Care Staff, 9, 48, 49
non-responsive institutions, 109
Code of Practice, 92
government documents, 92
positive workplace culture, 90–1
practitioners" steps, 92–3
UNISON, 91–2
working in, 92–3
non-verbal communication, 63

parental mental health issues, 19
performance management, 109
aim, 86
assessment, 98
care planning, 98
competence and accountability
frameworks, 96–7
core groups, 99
courts and care proceedings, 100
individual performance, 95
management of child protection
conferences, 99
management training, 97
monitoring and surveillance, 99
Newly Qualified Social Workers (NQSW), 96
organisational performance, 95, 97–8
positive publicity, 97
recording of incidents, 97
reports to child protection conferences, 98

resources and work environment, 97
and staff safety, 96
supervision training, 96
types, 95
workplace culture, 81
physical assault, 5
physiological responses to threats and violence,
17–19, 107, 108
automatic response, 18
fight, 18
flight, 18
freeze, 17–18
parasympathetic nervous system, 18
sympathetic nervous system, 18
planning interventions, 46–7
post-incident responses, 108
colleagues, support from, 78, 79
debriefing, 80
duty of care to staff, 79–81
impact, 76–7
management responses, 80–1
managers, support from, 78, 79–80
practitioners, 102
after the visit, 103
onsite, 102–3
preparations, 102
training and professional development, 102
professional/client relationship, 17
emphasis, 22
imbalance of power, 23
importance of, 22–3
question of power, 23
protection interventions, effectiveness of, 21
protective workers, and violence threat, 26
public expectation, 22
public transport, 32
publicity
adverse, 8
positive, 97

resistant families, 108
assertive approach, 52
justification, 83
maintaining focus, 85–7
recent concern, 84
resistance, types of, 83–4
strengths based approaches, 87
supervision, 85–7
use of intimidation and violence, 84
working with, 84–5
restorative practices, 87

risk assessments, 35
  of activities and situations, 36–7
  dangerousness checklist, 36
  of service users, 35–6

safe and effective working, 101, 109
  agencies/organisations, 104–5
  governments, 105
  inspectors, 105
  practitioners, 102–3
  supervisors, 103
  team, 104
safety
  awareness, 31–4, 107
  basic breakaway training, 72
  body language, using, 63–7
  in the car, 31–2
  in community locations, 35
  job design, 43
  in the office/interview room, 34
  organisations should protect staff, why, 42
  public transport, 32
  recording of incidents, 97
  resources, 97
  in service users' homes, 33–4
  staff policies, 38–9, 108
  staff training, 39
  in the street, 32
  training, 52–3
  travelling, 31
  work environment, 97
self-audit, 48
  action required, 50
  audit and review, 51–2
  legal responsibilities, 48
  policy, 48–9
  response to incidents, 51
  risk assessment, 49–50
self-protection, 39, 71, 72
Serious Case Review report, 8
single-agency working practices, 28, 52
Skills for Care, 9, 40, 92, 108
  advice for employers, 44
  Code of Practice, 44, 92
  leaflets, 92
social media, impact of, 3–4
Social Work Safety in the Workforce
    legislation, 109–10
social workers, lived experience of
  child and vulnerable adolescents, 11

consequences of issues, 12–13
impact of social media, 11–12
intimidation, 10
protective factors for, 13
system and resource issues, 12
threats, 10–11
violence, 11
statutory performance measures, 97
statutory powers, use of, 23
Stockholm syndrome, 25
strength-based approaches, 58, 87, 108
stress
  physiology of, 62–3
  and violence, 15
structural reorganisations, need for, 23
supervision, professional, 45–6
supervisors, 103
support programme, need for, 22
systems theory, 43

team, 104
teamwork
  building on training, 39
  responsibilities of staff, 40
  and staff safety, 38, 47
  team working, 13, 21, 47–8
threats
  lack of, 10, 16
  management, 88
  managing psychological impact, 16
  safety checklists, 22
  staff safety, 92
  supervision, 96
  through social media, 4
  topics, 44
trade union, 52
training, staff safety, 52–3
trauma, categories, 56
Trauma Informed Practice and Systemic
    Supervision, 45, 55–6
trauma-informed practice, 58–9, 83, 87, 108

UNISON, 91–2
United States, 6

Victorian study, 24, 28
violence and aggression, 55–6, 108
  addressing issues, 9
  affect on outcomes, 64
  aim of, 57

assertive responses, 70
baseline, 59–60
Batari's Box, 64–5
body language, 63–7, 69, 85, 108
breakaway training, 72
conflict management techniques, 67–9
crisis phase, 61
cycle of emotional arousal, 59–61, 67, 72–3
danger signs, 66–7
de-escalation techniques, 69–70, 71
domestic violence, 19
and emotional arousal, 59–61
escalation phase, 61, 69, 72
expressions of, 59
extent of, 3–5, 106–7
factors, 56–7
forms of, 16
Functional Behavioural Analysis, 57–8
goal of behaviour, 58
healthcare professionals, against, 6–7
immediate unexpected threats or
    aggression, 16
impact of, 5, 8, 11–12
implications for practice and employers, 28
keeping safe distance, 71
long-term intimidation, 17
management of, 65
minimisation of negative factors, 24
non-verbal communication, 63
physiology of stress, 62–3
post-crisis depression phase, 61

post-crisis reactions, 73–4
and power, 23
present situation, 9
realistic threats within relationship,
    10, 17
recovery phase, 61, 73
reporting rates, 9
responding assertively, 70
responses to, 17–19, 62–3
risk of, 6–7
self-protection, 71
Signs of Safety, 58
Strengthening Families, 58
supervision, 45
survey results, 3–6
techniques and approaches, 72–3
trigger phase, 60
triggers, 17
warning signs, 66
violent and aggressive families, working with,
    19–20
absent men, 19
atmosphere of violence, 20
domestic violence, 19
drugs and alcohol use, 19
father, role of, 19
frequency, 19
mother, focus on, 19–20

warning signs, 66
workplace violence, 6

Printed in the United States
by Baker & Taylor Publisher Services